Davis College of Business
JACKSONVILLE UNIVERSITY

As members of the dissertation committee, we the undersigned approve of this dissertation, ENTREPRENEURSHIP IN THE UNITED STATES OF AMERICA: ANTECEDENTS AND CONSEQUENCES FOLLOWING THE GREAT RECESSION by James A. Simak defended on April 20, 2018.

Dr. Richard Cebula
Dissertation Chair

Dr. Robert Boylan
Dissertation Committee Member

Dr. Margaret Foley
Dissertation Committee Member

Accepted and approved on behalf of the University:

Chair of Economics and Finance Department

Director of Graduate Programs

Dean, Davis College of Business

ABSTRACT

This dissertation challenges entrepreneurial economics by proposing a novel model based on entrepreneurial outcomes and coincidental institutional quality indicators. The research empirically assesses the impacts of prominent entrepreneurial activities and their interaction with economic and personal freedoms to create financial benefit in the context of the declining U.S. dynamism following the Great Recession. This study decomposes and combines the Kauffman Index of Entrepreneurial Activity, the Economic Freedom of North America and the Freedom in the 50 States of America in relationship to U.S. economic outcomes. Random-effects estimations of a panel data set of publicly available data reflecting explanatory variables for the 50 states for the years 2008 through 2016 suggest that sustaining traditional main street business activity and increasing above-average growth of entrepreneurial businesses exercise a positive and statistically significant influence on state financial well-being. Empirical evidence is presented to support the hypothesis that financial prosperity results from positive entrepreneurial activity coincident with increasing economic freedom(s) after allowing for a variety of other factors, *ceteris paribus.* Labor freedom at the state level has the most significant influence on positive entrepreneurial outcomes. Neither the rate of startup activity alone nor changes in personal freedom are found to influence financial benefits from entrepreneurship for U.S. States. The estimation results suggest entrepreneurial activity explains approximately 32% of the variation in real per capita gross state product.

Keywords: entrepreneurship, economic freedom, labor freedom, economic welfare, positive entrepreneurial outcomes

Copyright Page

DEDICATION

I dedicate my dissertation2 to my family, my friends and my DBA cohort for their encouragement and support throughout this journey. My deepest appreciation to Theresa for always supporting my dreams and aspirations – Thank you for all the marbles!

ACKNOWLEDGMENTS

I would like to thank the members of my dissertation advisory committee, Dr. Richard Cebula, Dr. Robert Boylan, and Dr. Maggie Foley, for their guidance and assistance in completing my doctoral studies and this dissertation. I must also thank the many outstanding professors and staff at Jacksonville University for their guidance and challenging me to think differently to grow as a new academic researcher. I greatly appreciate and acknowledge the support of Jerry, Jean, and Jeff at Harris Computer for helping me achieve this personal "dream". Lastly, a special thank you to Mr. Ray Parello for instilling in me an appreciation for higher education and his constant encouragement to complete my doctorate.

TABLE OF CONTENTS

Abstract.. iii

Dedication... v

Acknowledgments.. vi

List of Tables ix

CHAPTER ONE: INTRODUCTION 1

CHAPTER TWO: LITERATURE REVIEW...5

    Defining Entrepreneurship..5

    Theoretical Frameworks: Market Equilibrium versus Entrepreneurship 6

    Entrepreneurship as an Institutional Antecedent to Economic Well-being.................7

    Freedom as an Institutional Moderator of Entrepreneurship 9

CHAPTER THREE: METHODOLOGY 13

    The Research Question 15

        Economic Benefits: Real Per Capita Gross State Product 16

        Entrepreneurship and Entrepreneurial Activities..17

        Economic Freedom as Institutional Quality and Policy Indicator..........................21

        Freedom in the 50 States 26

        State-specific Control Variables 27

        Econometric Methods 29

    The Theoretical Model...30

CHAPTER FOUR: FINDINGS...34

    Results...35

    Hypotheses 37

    Ancillary Test Results..45

    Multicolinearity Tests 48

    Robustness Tests 51

CHAPTER FIVE: CONCLUSIONS..54

    Summary 54

    Discussion 55

    Implications...56

    Limitations 59

    Recommendations for Future Research 59

Appendices 61
    Appendix A 61
    Appendix B 65
References...67

LIST OF TABLES

Table 3.1 Descriptions of Variables...14

Table 3.2 Kauffman Index of Entrepreneurial Activity 18

Table 3.3 EFNA Subnational Indices...23

Table 3.4 Hausman Test Results..32

Table 4.1 Random Effects Semi-Log Results...36

Table 4.2 Random Effects Log-log Results..37

Table 4.3 Indicator Decomposition..39

Table 4.4 EFNA Subnational Estimates...41

Table 4.7 Ancillary Test Results..43

Table 4.5 Ancillary Results 46

Table 4.6 Additional Ancillary Results..47

Table 4.8 Variance Inflation Factor (VIF) Test Results...49

Table 4.9 Robustness Test Removing Regressors 51

Table 4.10 Robustness Tests Adding Regressors 52

Table 4.11 Robustness Test without Variables, AK and HI...53

CHAPTER ONE: INTRODUCTION

Entrepreneurship has been the object of extensive research and empirical study in recent years, with these inquiries covering a wide range of the theoretical landscape, including economics, psychological, social and management research. Schumpeter suggested entrepreneurship as the essential criteria for business and economic success almost a century ago (Backhaus & Schumpeter, 2003). This perspective of entrepreneurship as a critical function has endured and suggests the pursuit of entrepreneurial opportunities is a fundamental and essential phenomenon associated with an enduring free-market economy (Drucker, 1985).

There has been extensive research on the diverse dimensions and antecedents of entrepreneurship at the firm and micro-economic level, but economists have largely overlooked entrepreneurial activity as a primary driver of economic welfare. Acknowledgment of entrepreneurship as a contributing cause of economic prosperity is relatively recent, and most of the prior work by economists has been theoretical (Bjørnskov & Foss, 2016). The majority of economic research has primarily focused on static equilibrium theories, which underrepresent entrepreneurship as the dynamic engine of economic wellbeing in today's developed world (Cebula, Hall, Mixon, & Payne, 2015; Parker, 2015). Holcombe posits that economic progress is the product of positive entrepreneurship that enhances economic welfare (Cebula et al., 2015).

At the same time, recent economic trends of declining new business formation and new firm job growth suggest decreasing dynamism related to entrepreneurial activity (Decker, Haltiwanger, Jarmin, & Miranda, 2014). Historically, young businesses account for 20 percent of gross job creation with early-stage businesses creating almost 50 percent of new jobs (Haltiwanger, Jarmin, & Miranda, 2012). Following the great recession of 2008, the U.S. and the majority of states incurred a jobless recovery and decline in new business formation, reaching a new and significant level in the U.S., suggesting a profound structural change and a new form of stagnation (Burger & Schwartz, 2018). Economic progress, or the lack thereof, occurs because of entrepreneurship, which is also dependent upon institutional policies that encourage positive entrepreneurial activity in any well-functioning market economy (Cebula et al., 2015). A structural decline in entrepreneurship in the last decade is evident given the increase in early-stage firm failure rates, an exception being the most mature firms aged 16 years or more (Hathaway & Litan, 2014). This new "low" in observable entrepreneurial activity suggests institutional effects may not be promoting entrepreneurship, which correlates with the United States' declining economic freedom relative to the rest of the world over the last decade (Burger & Schwartz, 2018). Recent findings suggest institutional quality plays a significant role in economic wellbeing and influences how entrepreneurship is promoted, pursued and manifested. Institutions both advance entrepreneurial activity and may make the entrepreneurial activity more productive. The economics research and management literature have only recently studied institutional and policy effects on entrepreneurship (Bo, et al., 2013; Bjørnskov & Foss, 2016; Hall & Lawson, 2014; Parker, 2005). However, exactly which institutional dimensions are more or less important with respect to entrepreneurship and economic well-being remains an area of growing interest and debate (Bjørnskov & Foss, 2016; Hall & Lawson, 2014).

The extant empirical research on entrepreneurial economics has largely been limited to piece-wise studies of economic outcomes based on entrepreneurship, entrepreneurship and institutional quality relationships, and economic outcomes related to institutional quality (Hall & Lawson, 2014). Holcombe recently called for a better understanding of economic progress by acknowledging entrepreneurship as the primary economic engine and by promoting institutional policies that foster entrepreneurship (Cebula et al., 2015). Parker highlights several economic "unknowns" related to entrepreneurial economics and suggests greater focus on entrepreneurship as an important and emerging area of economics research. Answering these challenges begins with a more unified empirical understanding of entrepreneurial-economic outcomes and their prerequisite or coincident institutional influences. This research objective is consistent with the call by economists for a more dynamic and econometric understanding of economic welfare related to entrepreneurial activity and institutional influences.

The research question for this study is to empirically assess the impacts of prominent entrepreneurial activities and their interaction with institutional antecedents on the economic well-being within the United States. There has been a minimal amount of progress on systematically linking the prerequisites for entrepreneurship, entrepreneurial activity, and the aggregate consequences of both, into a single framework (Bjørnskov & Foss, 2016). Empirically studying this entrepreneurial-institutional–growth "trinity" at the U.S. subnational level can make a material contribution to the body of research, as this area has not been extensively studied or understood following the "Great Recession" (Rich, 2018). Confirmatory results may suggest probative guidance for academic researchers, as well as practitioners, and provide new directions for entrepreneurial activities and supporting policies to improve economic well-being. More generally, this researcher aspires to identify what specific entrepreneurial activities produce positive financial outcomes as moderated and mediated by localized institutional policies in the United States of America.

This dissertation consists of five chapters. In this introductory chapter, an introduction to the research problem and research question has been presented. Chapter Two summarizes the relevant literature and prior research underlying this study. Chapter Three develops the main hypotheses for empirical study and describes the explanatory variables, ancillary hypotheses, and modeling and panel-data analysis methods. Chapter Four presents the empirical results from random-effect estimations of publicly-available data reflecting explanatory variables for entrepreneurial outcomes and influences at the subnational level of the United States for years

2008-2016. Chapter Five summarizes the results of the research and provides guidance and future

research implications for this project. The supporting data, descriptive statistics, and references are

provided in the appendices.

CHAPTER TWO: LITERATURE REVIEW

Defining Entrepreneurship

Part of the challenge of studying entrepreneurship, in part, is defining entrepreneurship across the diverse academic research landscape. Ireland defines entrepreneurship as "innovativeness, risk-taking and proactive behaviors" (Ireland, Hitt, & Sirmon, 2003). Entrepreneurship is broader and should conceptualize a propensity to engage in "the pursuit of market opportunities" (Hult & Ketchen, 2001). Significant research also supports a foundational relationship between markets and entrepreneurship (Hurley & Hult, 1998; Jaworski & Kohli, 1993; Narver & Slater, 1990). Additionally, management theory's explanation of entrepreneurship includes environments and institutions as part of the overall phenomenon of entrepreneurship (Matsuno, Mentzer, & Ozsomer, 2002).

The micro-level concept of entrepreneurship is best conceptualized as a proclivity to recognize opportunities, take risks and be proactive in the creation of new ideas and behaviors that create value when acted upon (Cunningham & Lischeron, 1991). The bias for action and to "exploit" can be observed and measured across all levels of prior research (Scott & Venkataraman, 2001). This action-oriented entrepreneurship has also been found to be one of the most significant determinants of financial performance and wealth-creation (Burgelman, 1983; Crossan & Apaydin, 2010). For the purposes of this study, entrepreneurship will be defined as a productive, performance-based "output" associated with diverse and early-stage business activity, actualized by the Kauffman Index of Entrepreneurial Activity. This focused definition of entrepreneurship encompasses activities and behaviors that "exploit" opportunities and can be measured in hindsight from economic data. This treatment captures productive entrepreneurial behaviors and outcomes consistent with Baumol, as well as Schumpeter, while omitting nascent activity or intentions that have yet to create any measurable financial value.

Theoretical Frameworks: Market Equilibrium versus Entrepreneurship

Research of entrepreneurship has varied greatly from the study of individual characteristics of entrepreneurs to management schools of thought and economic theory (Bo et al., 2013; Burgelman, 1983; Gartner, Carland, Hoy, & Carland, 1988; McKenzie, Ugbah, & Smothers, 2007; Parker & Parker, 2009). There has been extensive management research on the various dimensions and antecedents of entrepreneurship at the individual, firm and micro-economic levels, which has largely gone unleveraged by economists. Although the activities of entrepreneurs and their effect on economic outcomes have long been suggested, most of the prior work by economists related to entrepreneurship and economic welfare has been theoretical (Bjørnskov & Foss, 2016; Parker, 2005). The majority of economic research has largely ignored entrepreneurship as the dynamic engine of economic prosperity in today's developed world (Cebula et al., 2015).

Classical scholars have focused on the dimensions of entrepreneurship as functions of; disruption (Backhaus & Schumpeter, 2003), new firm formation (Knight & Cavusgil, 2004), equilibrium (Kirzner, 1973), market creation (Bjørnskov & Foss, 2016; Casson, 1982). Parker (2005) provides a comprehensive review of mainly static economic theories related to entrepreneurship including: occupational choice, risk and return, credit rationing, asymmetric information, borrowing constraints, technology dispersion, human capital, and firm maturity. These approaches have most frequently conceptualized entrepreneurship as an occupational choice influenced by labor freedom (Parker, 2005). Baumol defines entrepreneurship as either one of positive economic contribution or a negative response to unintentional or misguided institutional policies, and further suggests that "positive" entrepreneurial activity is far more critical for economic growth than efficiency (Baumol, 1990; Baumol, 2002).

Empirically assessing direct economic benefits from entrepreneurship, and systematically linking institutional antecedents of the entrepreneurial activities is underrepresented by the majority of

6

prior work (Cebula et al., 2015; Parker & Parker, 2009). Bjørnskov and Foss (2016) synthesize current empirical understanding suggesting entrepreneurial activity has positive long-run economic consequences in terms of wealth and growth, whereby institutions can both promote entrepreneurship and make entrepreneurial activities more productive (Bjørnskov & Foss, 2016). The complex relationships and interactions between economic welfare, entrepreneurship and institutional quality remains an area of limited research requiring greater understanding. Holcombe calls for placing entrepreneurship at the center of economic progress and, at the same time, including the institutional antecedents as part of any credible analysis (Cebula et al., 2015).

Entrepreneurship as an Institutional Antecedent to Economic Well-being

Prior research suggests that entrepreneurial activity is necessary for long-term economic growth, and the majority of research on entrepreneurship as a contributing cause of economic growth has been theoretical (Bjørnskov & Foss, 2016). Economic research suggests that entrepreneurship and economic growth are positively related, and entrepreneurial activity benefits the economy at industry, regional, and national levels (Parker & Parker, 2009). Hafer reinforces a relationship between economic growth, entrepreneurship and economic freedom, finding significant evidence supporting a positive relationship between economic growth and entrepreneurship, with the body of prior work relating economic freedom and growth (Cebula et al., 2015). Wiseman and Young (2013) find that per-capita income is influenced by entrepreneurial activity at the state level, with economic freedom acting as a significant moderator of entrepreneurship (Wiseman & Young, 2013). Entrepreneurship is one of the most important sources of economic growth (Gwartney, Holcombe, & Lawson, 2004; Holcombe, 1998), and may explain a substantial proportion of variation in national growth rates (Powell & Weber, 2013).

By the start of the 21st century, there was general agreement that the majority of jobs in the developed world come from small firms (Parker, 2005). Haltiwanger (2006) finds job growth historically correlates with firm maturity with almost net job growth coming from early establishments less than two years old (Parker & Parker, 2009). Recent literature documents a decline in various measures of business dynamism related to entrepreneurship in the US, with firm failure rates increasing for each of the firm-age categories except for those aged 16 years or more over the last decade (Hathaway & Litan, 2014). Additionally, Burger and Schwartz find state-level jobless recoveries to be a prevalent trend at the state level following the Great Recession of 2008 and suggest the rate of entrepreneurial activity is a significant predictor of jobless recoveries (Burger & Schwartz, 2018). Understanding the emerging impact or lack thereof from entrepreneurship should be a high priority, given the vital role early high-growth businesses have historically played in the US economy (Decker, Haltiwanger, Jarmin, & Miranda, 2016a).

As previously highlighted, empirical understanding of entrepreneurship as the force behind our economic well-being is under-represented in economics research (Cebula et al., 2015). And, there has been little work to systematically link entrepreneurial activity, its economic benefits and institutional influences in a comprehensive empirical model (Bjørnskov & Foss, 2016; Parker, 2005). Defining causality and robust relationships is difficult because of the complex interaction and mutually reinforcing nature of these inter-related forces. Bjørnskov & Foss highlight the dynamics of entrepreneurship as both a cause and a consequence of economic outcomes as entrepreneurship is born out of necessity in a downturn and driven by growth in an upturn (Bjørnskov & Foss, 2008). Audretsch and Acs find that entrepreneurial activity increases with economic growth as a growing economy creates more opportunity (Acs, Audretsch, & Feldman, 1994). In contrast, several empirical studies posit the opposite effect finding entrepreneurial activity influences long-run growth and productivity (Bjørnskov & Foss, 2013). Overall, the causes and consequences of entrepreneurship lack solid evidence based on econometric analysis (Parker, 2005).

Freedom as an Institutional Moderator of Entrepreneurship

Institutions can advance entrepreneurial activity and influence positive economic outcomes, in the long run. North's seminal work on the influence of institutions on the economy is the basis for the majority of research on economic freedom and institutional quality (North, 1990; North, 1991). Economists and management scholars have only recently focused attention on understanding these influences on entrepreneurial activities as called for in this study (Baumol, 1990; Bjørnskov & Foss, 2016; Bradley & Klein, 2016; Holcombe, 1998; Sobel, 2008; Stansel, Torra, & McMahon, 2017; Zahra & Wright, 2011). Economic Freedom has emerged as the accepted measure of institutional quality in economic research at the global, regional, national and local levels, with the majority of studies finding increasing institutional quality has a wide variety of positive outcomes (Hall & Lawson, 2014). Economic freedom may both moderate and mediate the effects of entrepreneurship on financial performance, but understanding which institutional policy dimensions are most important is an area for much-needed research (Bjørnskov & Foss, 2016; Parker, 2005).

Economic freedom is defined herein as "*the fundamental right of every human to control his or her own labor and property. In economically free societies, individuals are free to work, produce, consume, and invest in any way they please, where governments enable labor, capital, and goods to move freely, and refrain from undue coercion or constraint*" (Miller, Kim, & Roberts, 2018). In the majority of research, economic freedom is actualized as indicators of institutional quality and policy. The seminal work of Gwartney, Block, and Lawson on economic freedom produced the Economic Freedom of the World (EFW) index, which has become the accepted measurement for economic research in global studies (Gwartney, Lawson, Block, & Fraser, 1996). This EFW index has been used in hundreds of studies to show a positive relationship between institutional quality described by economic freedom and various economic outcomes (Gwartney,

2009; Gwartney, Lawson, & Hall, 2017). The Economic Freedom of North America (EFNA) enables study of the influences of economic freedom at the sub-national level across North America and was based on the same methodology as EFW (Stansel et al., 2017).

EFNA has been widely used in hundreds of peer-reviewed studies as an indicator of institutional quality at both the national and subnational levels (Stansel et al., 2017). More recent papers confirm a positive correlation between economic freedom and entrepreneurship throughout the U.S. states (Powell & Weber, 2013). The EFNA index is comprised of components covering three main areas: government spending, taxation, and labor market freedom (Stansel et al., 2017). For the subnational indices, EFNA excludes EFW dimensions for legal and property rights, sound money policies, and international trade, which are usually found to be the most significant influences in global and world comparative studies (Stansel et al., 2017). EFNA's subnational indices for the United States enable more useful comparison of the influences of economic freedoms at the individual state level as used in this study (Stansel et al., 2017).

Economic freedom at the subnational level has been found to be positively associated with a variety of measures of economic welfare and entrepreneurial activity (Stansel et al., 2017). Since the publication of EFNA in 2002, more than 230 peer-reviewed academic articles have employed it to study the relationships between institutional policies and other indicators such as per capita economic growth and entrepreneurial activity (Cebula et al., 2015; Hall & Lawson, 2014; Stansel et al., 2017). Hall and Lawson (2014) surveyed the existing literature and overwhelmingly found economic freedom has positive effects on economic growth, entrepreneurship, jobs, productivity and other macroeconomic outcomes (Hall & Lawson, 2014). Powell & Weber recently found economic freedom is robustly related with a higher rate of business formation in the United States using composite indices for EFNA and KIEA (Powell &

Weber, 2013). The EFNA subnational indices will best support this investigation into the relationship between entrepreneurship and economic well-being as moderated by economic freedom via econometric testing. This research is still needed to provide meaningful insight into the impacts of regulation and policy on entrepreneurship (Parker, 2005)

As an alternative to EFNA, the CATO Institute's Freedom in the Fifty States (US50) index provides a "total" freedom index as an indicator of institutional quality in the United States (Ruger & Sorens, 2017b). The US50 index was created by Ruger & Sorens and is differentiated from Frazer's EFNA index because it adds a personal freedom dimension to economic freedom indicators for fiscal and regulatory policies. This personal freedom dimension consists of the wide array of state-level policies and regulations related to: guns, alcohol, marijuana, travel, gaming, mala prohibita and miscellaneous civil liberties, education, civil asset forfeiture, crime, marriage rights, campaign finance, and tobacco (Ruger & Sorens, 2017b). Ruger & Sorens' index does not weight the subcomponents equally as does EFNA but assembles the underlying variables according to the value or cost to those people whose freedoms are affected. The US50 index has been used in multiple studies as an alternative to EFNA because of the flexibility to change weightings and study the proposed personal freedom dimension.

Hall et al., (2013) finds that the overall effect of freedom on entrepreneurial activity is positive and statistically significant, with economic freedom and not personal freedom having a significant influence on entrepreneurial outcomes (Hall, Nikolaev, Pulito, & Van Metre, 2013). Campbell and Rogers (2007) find a positive relationship between economic freedom and net business formation (Campbell & Rogers, 2007). Beaulier and Sutter (2013) suggest economic freedom and growth are related to entrepreneurial activity at the international and state level (Beaulier & Sutter, 2013). Campbell et al (2013) finds that economic freedom is not always a robust indicator of entrepreneurship at the state level (Campbell, Mitchell, & Rogers, 2013b).

Powell and Weber (2013) assess an earlier version of KIEA and find that the size of government is inversely related to the level of business formation (Powell & Weber, 2013).

In general, research consistently finds increasing economic freedom to be associated with greater levels of entrepreneurship (Hall et al., 2013). This literature continues to expand rapidly, but only a small fraction of this research explores the direct relationships between entrepreneurship and institutional quality as defined by economic and personal freedom(s) (Hall & Lawson, 2014). For the purposes of this study, the EFNA indices will be used to assess economic freedom(s), and US50 index for Personal Freedom dimension will be added as an ancillary explanatory variable.

CHAPTER THREE: METHODOLOGY

The main hypotheses for empirical study are developed in this chapter, providing a detailed description of the explanatory variables, control variables, and the associated panel-data analysis methods. The econometric framework is designed to explain the aggregate economic benefits of entrepreneurial activities at the state level, and link entrepreneurial activity with economic freedom in a single empirical model. The data used for the estimations with their description and sources are presented in Table 3.1. The descriptive statistics for all data used in this study are presented in the Table A.1 in the Appendix.

The study is the first to leverage the most recent incarnation of the Kauffman Index of Entrepreneurial Activity (KIEA) and decompose entrepreneurial activity into three (or more) tractable comparative measures, e.g. traditional small business, startups, and high-growth ventures. This study also employs the subcomponents of the EFNA index to systematically link these prominent entrepreneurial activities directly to actionable institutional policy. Additional socio-economic factors that influence financial outcomes in relation to entrepreneurial activity and institutional influences are used. The general model is expressed as:

Economic Benefit = f(entrepreneurial activities, institutional policies,

socio-economic factors)

Economic benefit is defined as a dynamic function of productive entrepreneurial activities, institutional policies and social-economic-demographic determinants. Real per capita gross state product will be used as a proxy for aggregate economic benefits at the state level. Entrepreneurial activities are captured by the KIEA main street, startup and high-growth indices. Socio-economic-demographic factors include unemployment, educational attainment and personal freedom. Institutional policies are incorporated through the EFNA subnational area components.

Table 3.1 Descriptions of Variables

Variable	Description	Source
PCREAL_GSP	Annual Real Gross State Product Per Capita –used as an indicator of economic welfare and benchmark	U.S. Dept. of Commerce U.S. Bureau of Economic Analysis, State Data
STARTUP_INDEX	KIEA Index of Startup Activity as composite index comprised of the; Rate of New Entrepreneurs, the Opportunity Share of New Entrepreneurs, and Startup Density	2017 Kauffmann Index of Entrepreneurial Activity www.kaufmann.org
MAINSTREET_INDEX	KIEA Index of Main Street Entrepreneurship is an equally weighted index of; the number of established small businesses, the survival rate of companies, and the number of business owners in a state	2017 Kauffmann Index of Entrepreneurial Activity www.kaufmann.org
GROWTH_INDEX	Kauffman Index of Growth Entrepreneurship is an equally weighted index of the; Rate of Startup Growth, Share of Scaleups, and High Growth Company Density	2017 Kauffmann Index of Entrepreneurial Activity www.kaufmann.org
EFNA_OVERALL_SUBN	Economic Freedom of North America Index - State Index for United States - Subnational Indices	Dean Stansel, José Torra, and Fred McMahon. 2016. www.fraserinstitute.org
EFNA_A1_SUBN	Economic Freedom of North America Index - State Index Component Area 1 - Size of Government	Dean Stansel, José Torra, and Fred McMahon. 2016. www.fraserinstitute.org
EFNA_A2_SUBN	Economic Freedom of North America Index - State Index Component Area 2 - Taxation	Dean Stansel, José Torra, and Fred McMahon. 2016. www.fraserinstitute.org
EFNA_A3_SUBN	Economic Freedom of North America Index - State Index Component Area 3 – Regulation (Labor Freedom)	Dean Stansel, José Torra, and Fred McMahon. 2016. www.fraserinstitute.org
US50_PERSONAL	US50 Personal Freedom Index	Ruger & Sorens. 2016. *Freedom in The 50 States*, www.freedominthe50states.org
UNEMP_RATE	Annual State Unemployment Rate derived from U.S. Bureau of Labor Statistics annual unemployment rate for the 50 states.	U.S. Dept. of Commerce U.S. Bureau of Economic Analysis, State Data
P_HIGH_ONLY	Derived from "Percent of Persons 25 Years and Over Who Have Completed High School (Includes Equivalency)," less P_BACH to estimate High School or equivalency Only attainment.	U.S. Census Bureau Educational Attainment Population Survey Table 13 2000-2016
P_BACH	"Percent of Persons 25 Years and Over Who Have Completed a Bachelor's Degree,"	U.S. Census Bureau Educational Attainment Population Survey Table 13 2000-2016

The Research Question

Do the independent variables describing distinct entrepreneurial activities and the supporting institutional policies at the state level exhibit a positive and statistically significant impact on economic welfare, specifically financial benefit in terms of real per capita gross state product, when controlling for socio-economic-demographic influences as hypothesized?

H1: STARTUP ACTIVITY WILL HAVE A POSITIVE AND STATISTICALLY SIGNIFICANT EFFECT ON REAL_GSP, *ceteris paribus*

H2: MAINSTREET ACTIVITY WILL HAVE A POSITIVE AND STATISTICALLY SIGNIFICANT EFFECT ON REAL_GSP, *ceteris paribus*

H3: GROWTH ACTIVITY WILL HAVE A POSITIVE AND STATISTICALLY SIGNIFICANT EFFECT ON REAL_GSP, *ceteris paribus*

H4: ECONOMIC AND PERSONAL FREEDOM WILL HAVE A POSITIVE AND STATISTICALLY SIGNIFICANT EFFECT ON REAL_GSP, *ceteris paribus*

Ancillary research questions will consider whether the following independent control variables exhibit expected positive (negative) and statistically significant influence on REAL_GSP, *ceteris paribus*, for consistency with previous empirical studies as follows.

Ha: UNEMP_RATE will have a meaningful and statistically significant effect, *ceteris paribus*

Hb: BACH_DEG will have a positive and statistically significant effect, *ceteris paribus*

Hc: HIGH_ONLY will have a positive and statistically significant effect, *ceteris paribus*

For robustness testing, additional socio-economic variables common in the literature will be estimated including the following: state population growth, immigration, net migration, and average January temperature. Per capita personal income and real median household income will be assessed as additional measures of economic benefits for consistency with the findings for REAL_GSP and prior research. The variables, sources, methodology, and derivations of data used in this study's estimations are herein described.

Economic Benefits: Real Per Capita Gross State Product

The dependent variable and benchmark of primary interest to be used in this study is Real Per Capita Gross State Product (REAL_GSP), which serves as a useful indicator of economic welfare and provides a highly useful measure of the quality of life at the state level (Cebula et al., 2015; Oulton, 2012). For our purposes, Gross State Product is considered the "value-added" state counterpart of the nation's GDP as defined by the U.S. Department of Commerce, Bureau of Economic Analysis (United & Bureau of Economic, 2006). GSP estimates are measured as the sum of the distributions by industry and state of the components of gross domestic income, and it is noted that Gross State Product and Gross Domestic Product are not equivalent at the national level. (United & Bureau of Economic, 2006). Because state-level GDP estimates are interpolated based on the U.S. national estimates in non-benchmark years, real per capita GSP will be used as a labeling convention in this study but should be considered synonymous for comparative reference to U.S. state-level real per capita GDP in prior empirical studies. It should be stressed that nowhere in this study (or, in general in related studies) has the state-level measure of income or gross state product been scaled by state-level living-cost indices.

The objective of this study is to estimate the contributions of specific entrepreneurial activities and related institutional policies on positive financial outcomes, not to define a comprehensive model for GSP. Recent studies have successfully used GDP measures as an indicator of economic benefit including Cebula, Clark, and Mixon (2013) and Wiseman and Young (2013). Additionally, Plehn-Dujowich finds that entrepreneurship has an inverted U relationship with economic outcomes, and the relationship between entrepreneurship and related economic benefits may not necessarily hold when including unemployment as an explanatory variable (Plehn-Dujowich & Grove, 2012). Accordingly, this study's empirical specifications will use the logarithm of per capita real gross state product as the dependent variable in estimates to account for non-linear effects. The explanatory and control variables will be adjusted appropriately to support both semi-log and log-log specifications of the theoretical model(s). Appropriate social-economic control variables are added at the state level to be consistent with prior research.

Entrepreneurship and Entrepreneurial Activities

Campbell suggests a variety of independent variables under the general heading of "entrepreneurial activity" and calls for researchers to put greater effort into conceptualizing entrepreneurship (Campbell, Mitchell, & Rogers, 2013a). The measurement of entrepreneurship is a compromise between theoretical perspectives and available measures, and most studies use either survey-based measures for new firm formation or self-employment, which do not capture (Schumpeterian) entrepreneurial activities of established firms nor nascent (Kirznerian) activities of individuals (Bjørnskov & Foss, 2016). The latest Kauffman Index of Entrepreneurial Activity has some advantages over previous measures of entrepreneurship (Hall & Sobel, 2008), and captures the dynamic nature of entrepreneurial activity and its relationship to current conditions (Baughn, Neupert, & Sugheir, 2013).

For the purposes of addressing the aforementioned issues in this study, the Kauffman Index of Entrepreneurial Activity will be decomposed into the subcomponent indices representing each of the three unique activity areas by state and by year. The recently introduced Growth and Main Street sub-indices have not been used widely in research and provide this research with a new and comprehensive set of comparative indicators for describing small business formation, growth, and longevity across the spectrum of entrepreneurial activities at the state level. Although the KIEA composite index exists for each state going back before 2000, the preference for using the diversity found in the recent area sub-indices limits the timeframe to 2008 through 2016 following the most recent recession. The Kauffman Index of

Entrepreneurship (KIEA) provides a balanced perspective of entrepreneurship across the U.S. states, and the use of the new area indices provide unique indicators across both geography and time not previously incorporated in research (Morelix & Russell-Fritch, 2018). The KIEA area indices and their underlying subcomponents and contributing factors are described in the Table 3.2 below.

Table 3.2 Kauffman Index of Entrepreneurial Activity

	KIEA Startup Index	KIEA Mainstreet Index	KIEA Growth Index
Subcomponent Description	**Rate of New Entrepreneurs**; The percentage of adults transitioning into entrepreneurship at a given point in time	**Rate of Business Owners**; The total number of business owners in a location at a given point in time	**Rate of Startup Growth**; The average growth of a cohort of new startups in their first five years
	Opportunity Share of New Entrepreneurs; The percentage of new entrepreneurs driven primarily by "opportunity" vs. "necessity"	**Established Small Business Density**; The number of businesses older than five years with less than fifty employees normalized by population	**Share of Scaleups**; The number of small businesses that grew to employ at least fifty people by their tenth year of operation as a percentage of all businesses ten years and younger
	Startup Density; The number of new employer businesses normalized by population		**High-Growth Company Density**; The number of fast-growing companies with at least 2 million dollars in annual revenue normalized by business population

The KIEA Startup Activity Index (STARTUP_INDEX) subcomponent is an indicator of early entrepreneurial activity, encompassing new firm formation, market opportunity, and startup density (Russell et al., 2016). The Main Street Index (MAINSTREET_INDEX) subcomponent was added in 2015 to add a dimension for traditional small business ownership and density of established, local businesses (Russell, Morelix, Fairlie, & Reedy, 2015). The Growth Index

18

(GROWTH_INDEX) subcomponent was added in 2016 to provide a complete picture of entrepreneurial activities in the U.S. by including high-growth, early stage business activity (Russell, Morelix, Fairlie, & Reedy, 2017). These indices measure positive entrepreneurial activity and contribution by design and construction (Russell, Morelix, Fairlie, & Reedy, 2016). The recent addition of the Main Street and Growth indices overcomes limitations associated with using the previous KIEA index primarily as a proxy for new sole-proprietorships (Powell & Weber, 2013). KIEA best identifies the outcome-based change in entrepreneurial activities and overcomes previous limitations as an indicator of positive, impactful entrepreneurship (Mann & Shideler, 2015).

The KIEA Startup Index is a novel and comprehensive indicator of all types of new and early business activity at the state level (employers, non-employers, unincorporated, and incorporated businesses) and is derived from the U.S. Census Bureau's Current Population Survey (Russell et al., 2016). It captures the Rate of New Entrepreneurs in the economy as the percentage of adults becoming entrepreneurs in a given month and devoting 15 hours or more a week to working in the business. This index tends to under-report startup activity because it excludes very early nascent entrepreneurial activities such as "side-gigs." It also captures the Opportunity Share of New Entrepreneurs, defined as the percentage of individuals who start a business for opportunity rather than out of necessity. The Startup Index also includes Startup Density, defined as the rate at which businesses less than one-year-old with one or more employees are created (Russell et al., 2016). The components for Rate of New Entrepreneurs and the Opportunity Share of New Entrepreneurs are calculated on three-year moving averages to reduce sampling issues. These indices provide a better instrument for measuring early entrepreneurial activity as compared to survey-based approaches such as Global Entrepreneurship Monitor's Total early-stage Entrepreneurial Activity (Stead, Worrell, & Stead, 1990), which is one of the commonly cited measures of entrepreneurial activity (Díaz-Casero, Coduras, & Hernández-Mogollón, 2012).

The KIEA Mainstreet Index provides a comprehensive, normalized indicator of small business activity in the local U.S. economy, and this firm-level data is derived from an expansive dataset from the Census Bureau's Current Population Survey and U.S. Census Business Dynamics Statistics covering approximately five million businesses (Russell et al., 2015). As such, there are no sampling issues with this Mainstreet Index. This index is an equally weighted measure of three normalized subcomponents; the Rate of Business Owners calculated as the percentage of adults that own a business, the Survival Rate of firms calculated as the percentage of firms that have currently survived for five years, and the Established Small Business Density as the ratio of established small employer businesses to the total number of firms (Russell et al., 2015). Incorporating these main street components in empirical analysis allows this study to model both business owners and the businesses they own (Russell et al., 2015).

The KIEA Growth Index measures high-growth, entrepreneurial business activity across all firms and industries in the United States based on annual revenue growth and job creation thresholds, which is derived from U.S. Census Bureau data and private data from the Inc. Magazine's annual Inc. 500|5000 list of high-growth companies (Russell et al., 2017). The Growth index is an equally weighted measure of three normalized subcomponents: the Rate of Startup Growth calculated as how much startups have grown on average in their first five years, the Share of Scaleups calculated as the percentage of businesses employing 50 or more people by their tenth year of operation, and High-Growth Density calculated as the ratio of private companies with at least 20 percent annualized growth over three years and at least two million dollars in annual revenues (Russell et al., 2017). Kauffman's approach is novel and partially derived from prior work on growth trajectories of new firms by Reedy and Litan (Russell et al. 2017).

The KIEA Growth Index highlights businesses we normally identify as "unicorns," but this measure encompasses both early-stage private companies as well as businesses that achieve or sustain high growth at later stages across many industries (Russell et al., 2017). The Growth Index is distinct and complementary to the Startup Index, which focuses only on new firm formation measures and location preference. This indicator has no sampling issues but can suffer from survivor bias because cohorts average all firm births with those that survive for five years (Russell et al., 2017). Although the KIEA exists for each state going back to 1996, these most recent subcomponents for startup, mainstreet and growth activities are limited to the study's years from 2008 to 2016. This is consistent with the focus on productive, performance-based entrepreneurial activity rather than the "inputs" (e.g., investment, patents, R&D expenses) often used in prior entrepreneurship research.

Economic Freedom as Institutional Quality and Policy Indicator

As previously discussed, this study posits entrepreneurship as a primary economic contributor, and considers institutional policies as essential influences to foster entrepreneurial activity. Institutional quality actualized as economic freedom must be included in any credible model of entrepreneurial economic progress (Cebula et al., 2015), and further research is called for to understand the direct impacts of regulation and policy on entrepreneurship (Parker, 2005). Economic Freedom is a widely accepted measure of institutional quality, and findings suggest several measures of economic freedom provide an effective proxy for institutional quality and its influence on economic well-being (Hall & Lawson, 2007). Economic freedom may both moderate and mediate the effects of entrepreneurship on economic performance, and consideration of the individual dimensions of economic freedom requires more study (Bjørnskov & Foss, 2016). The Economic Freedom of North America (EFNA) measures the extent to which the policies of individual states are supportive of economic freedom and the ability of individuals to act without undue economic restrictions (Stansel et al., 2017). Since the first publication of the Economic

Freedom of North America in 2002, more than 230 academic and policy articles have explored the

relationship between economic outcomes, entrepreneurial activity and this indicator of economic

freedom (Stansel et al., 2017).

The EFNA subnational indices use different variables and calculations that suit subnational

empirical study but are in theory no different than the EFW or similar indices used for cross-

country or global studies. The EFNA subnational indices exclude several criteria used in the

Economic Freedom of the World (EFW) including: Legal Systems and Property Rights, Sound

Money, and Freedom to Trade Internationally (Stansel et al., 2017). For comparison between the

U.S., Canada, and Mexico, the EFNA cross-country indices are expanded to include government

enterprises and investments, the top marginal income and payroll tax rates, and credit market and

business regulations (Stansel et al., 2017). For this study's comparisons of entrepreneurship within

the United States, the EFNA subnational indices are most appropriate and will be used (Stansel et

al., 2017). The EFNA subnational index will serve as an effective proxy of institutional quality at

the U.S. state level for empirical analysis.

This study will decompose and assess specific subnational EFNA subcomponents for a

more granular understanding of the relationships on economic outcomes in the United States. The

underlying EFNA methodology used at the subnational level promotes an objective ranking based

on three area measurements: 1) Size of Government 2) Taxation 3) Labor Market Freedoms

(Stansel et al., 2017). As such, only four of the ten EFNA economic freedom measures are

considered at the state and metro levels (Stansel et al., 2017). The EFNA indices use zero (0) to

ten (10) scales with higher values indicating the higher levels of economic freedom for each

subcomponent area, which are combined with equally weighting into an overall indicator of

economic freedom at the subnational level (Stansel et al., 2017). The EFNA subnational indices and their contributing subcomponents are listed in Table 3.3.

Table 3.3 EFNA Subnational Indices

EFNA Subnational Indices	Area Subcomponent Basis
EFNA Area 1 – Government Spending	Government Expenditures Transfers and Subsidies Social Security Payments
EFNA Area 2 - Taxation	Tax Revenue Top Marginal Personal Income Tax Rate Indirect Tax Revenue Sales Taxes
EFNA Area 3 - Labor Market Freedom	Minimum Wage Annual Income Government Employment (as Percentage of Total) Union Density

EFNA Area 1 encompasses Government Spending, which reduces economic freedom when spending exceeds the necessary level for protective and productive government function, and oversteps its role by providing goods and services that may be delivered by the private sector (Stansel et al., 2017). The Area 1 subcomponent is adjusted for state transfers and subsidies that reduce the real returns from private activity (Gwartney et al., 1996). Insurance and Retirement Payments are also included in the calculation to include government-mandated retirement and disability insurance programs that reduce economic freedom (Stansel et al., 2017). EFNA Area 2 is an indicator of the tax burdens and incentives on entrepreneurial activity. This area subcomponent is a relative indicator of the equally-weighted levels of income and payroll taxes, property taxes, sales tax and other business tax burdens within a state (Stansel et al., 2017). EFNA Area 3 encompasses regulatory influences on entrepreneurial activity at the subnational level (Stansel et al., 2017). Area 3 aggregates regulatory dimensions at the subnational level for: minimum wage legislation, government employment as a percentage of total state employment, and union density (Stansel et al., 2017). This EFNA component primarily provides an indicator of variation in labor market freedom across the United States.

This study emphasizes the more dynamic and tractable institutional influences on entrepreneurial activity at the subnational level and will use the most appropriate EFNA subcomponent as the primary indicator of economic freedom. Ashby suggests a positive relationship between entrepreneurship and institutional quality (Cebula et al., 2015). Sobel (2008) finds productive or positive entrepreneurial activity is positively related to EFNA at the state level. However, Powell and Weber find an earlier version of the KIEA index is insignificant in relation to economic freedom (Powell & Weber, 2013). Hafer suggests that economic freedom affects entrepreneurial activity on a more granular level and extends to economic performance (Cebula et al., 2015). Additionally, the correlation between the freedom subcomponents suggests possible multicollinearity and simultaneity may be a concern, so the selection of a specific "granular" measure will be necessary to assess which types of entrepreneurial activities stand out at the state level.

The Area 1 subcomponent highly correlates with the overall EFNA subnational index and the Area 3 Index, and selection of the explanatory variable for economic freedom must be balanced against possible interaction between KIEA, EFNA and the dependent variables used in this study. The subnational EFNA index excludes the top marginal income and payroll tax burdens, and the study assumes that the majority of the tax influences on entrepreneurial activity are imposed at the federal level. Krichevskiy and Snyder also find conflicting results related to the effects of taxation on entrepreneurship with both positive and negative influences (Krichevskiy & Snyder, 2015). As such, the EFNA area 2 subcomponent is not considered a high-value indicator for this study given the primacy of federal taxation and will be considered in the context of robustness testing. Goel suggests that positive entrepreneurship is identified by an increase in entrepreneurial outcomes when economic freedom increases, with labor freedom having the most significant influence on entrepreneurial activity (Cebula et al., 2015). Cebula and Alexander suggest increases in labor freedom influence labor force participation, which may also have a significant influence on entrepreneurial activity (Cebula et al., 2015). Stansel and Bolgna make important distinctions related to entrepreneurship based on the Area 3 component of EFNA and find that higher levels of government employment suggest the government is directly undertaking work that can be contracted privately, which causes private businesses and individuals to compete against their own tax dollars (Stansel et al.). Additionally, the minimum wage indicator in EFNA Area 3 serves as a valid measure for productivity differences between states (Stansel et al.).

The EFNA Area 3 index serves as a proxy for labor freedom, productivity and, to some degree, the overall entrepreneurial incentives or barriers at the state level. The minimum wage dimension measures the level of restriction on new entrants to the workforce, and also acts a proxy for the ability to pay wages and productivity differences between states (Stansel et al., 2017). The government employment dimension is calculated as a ratio of government employment to total state employment and indicates the level of labor the government is taking out of the market. This also indicates the degree to which the government is limiting and competing with the private sector and individuals in providing goods and services within the state. When the government directly undertakes activities that can be better delivered by established businesses, state economies move towards a quasi-monopoly (Stansel et al., 2017). The third dimension of EFNA Area 3 is union density, which measures unionization rates, which act as a proxy for enforcement of overall regulation on entrepreneurial activities (Stansel et al., 2017). At the subnational level, Area 3 excludes regulations commonly found influential at the national or global levels such as credit market and business regulations (Stansel et al., 2017). This study does not discount these critical dimensions and posits that the administrative and compliance costs of starting a business are largely heterogeneous throughout the United States.

In summary, the EFNA Area 3 index for Labor Freedom best represents economic freedom as a requisite influence and "red-tape" barrier to positive entrepreneurial activity. EFNA Area 3 captures both labor freedom, right to work influences and "competition" from state and local governments, which is a predominant factor for entrepreneurial contribution and freedom influences on per capita real gross state product. The EFNA subnational indices exclude "significant" economic freedom influences represented in prior work, but this study accepts these limitations, as these "global" freedom influences should be largely uniform at the state level, *ceteris paribus*. For this study, EFNA Area 3 will be used as the primary measure of economic freedom in the context of entrepreneurial activities and their related outcomes in terms of state-level financial outcomes.

Freedom in the 50 States

The Cato Institute's Freedom in the 50 U.S. States (US50) is a relatively new state-level freedom index developed by Ruger and Sorens (2016) and provides an alternative to EFNA for subnational U.S. freedom research. Ruger and Sorens define "freedom" as a moral concept - the ability to pursue one's ends without unjust interference from others (Ruger & Sorens, 2017a). The US50 provides an overall freedom index as a weighted total of subcomponent indices for economic freedom and personal freedom. Economic freedom is further decomposed into fiscal and regulatory indices. The weights used to calculate the economic and personal freedom indices are based on the estimated costs of government restrictions on each of their constituent parts. The overall freedom index is comprised of approximately equal thirds of the three major index components: fiscal policy, regulatory policy and personal freedom (Ruger & Sorens 2017a).

Ruger & Sorens' index is unique in that it ranks the U.S. states across economic and personal dimensions, and the personal freedom dimension is not represented in EFNA. The personal freedom index is based on a subjectively weighted composite of policy categories including; gun rights, alcohol rights, marijuana-related rights, travel policies, gaming policies, mala prohibita, education, asset forfeiture, crime, marriage policy, campaign finance policy, and tobacco policy. The Ruger and Sorens' index provides a robust representation of personal freedom at the state level (Cebula, 2014). As such, the personal freedom index component will be used in this study to further estimate "total" freedom influences on economic outcomes at the U.S. subnational level.

State-specific Control Variables

Economic freedom is not the only criteria for locating economic activity within the U.S. because all U.S. states share a similar (federal) institutional structure (Beaulier & Sutter, 2013). The prior work suggests a long list of appropriate controls to account for human-capital and state-level variation in GSP or similar measures of economic well-being. Given the focus on entrepreneurial outcomes and influences, human-capital controls are most appropriate for this study. There is quite a long list of potential measures that can be used as control variables to capture socio-economic and demographic regional variation. This study will select minimal control variables as a least common denominator from prior literature, selecting the unemployment rate and educational attainment as control variables (Powell & Weber, 2013). Cheung recommends that availability of human capital as the most significant influence on economic outcomes, with other traditionally considered variables such as population, R&D expenditure and patent activity to be less significant (Cheung, 2014).

Unemployment in the context of economic outcomes and entrepreneurial activity supports a more dynamic relationship, where entrepreneurial activity and economic growth are mutually re-enforcing (causal), and, at the same time mutually dampen unemployment (Plehn-Dujowich & Grove). This relationship is ambiguous given the startup activity rate as measured by employment has largely remained the same since the great recession (Haltiwanger et al., 2012). Hall (2013) prioritizes using the unemployment rate as a specific control variable and significant influence on entrepreneurship (Hall et al., 2013). Pearson et al. (2012) also find economic benefits are positively related to economic freedom with unemployment contributing a negative influence (Pearson, Nyonna, & Kim, 2012).

Parker (2004) shows that entrepreneurs tend to be more educated than non-entrepreneurs, and differences in human capital can be controlled using percent of the adult population with an advanced degree at the state level (Parker, 2004). This study will consider attainment of both bachelors' degrees and high school diplomas, specifically adjusting for high-school-only attainment by subtracting the percentage of the state population with bachelor's degrees from the percentage of the state population with a high school degree. Prior work has commonly used educational attainment to account for human-capital differences across states including; (Cebula et al., 2015; Hall & Sobel, 2008; Parker, 2004; Powell & Weber, 2013). The use of per capita measures for dependent variables and explanatory indicators adequately aggregate business "densities" at the state level so other control variables such as population density and population growth are less relevant. Other commonly used control variables including January average temperature, immigration, net migration, and immigrant share will be assessed as part of robustness testing for consistency with prior research.

Econometric Methods

The methodology of economics is the study of the relationship between theory and conclusions about the real world; methodology examines the ways in which economists justify theories and why they prefer one theory over another based on descriptive and prescriptive considerations (Salanti, Marchi, & Blaug, 1992) This study relies on robust observational and publicly-available data rather than data collected from controlled experiments, which is consistent with econometric methodology (Salanti et al., 1992). Due to the reliance on observational data rather than the use of controlled experiments, regression analysis is a commonly accepted statistical method of analysis. Econometrics may be used to characterize a relationship or phenomenon, which distinguishes the econometric methods used in this study from statistics in that the focus is on establishing causation, while statistics is content with correlation (Heckman, 2000).

This dissertation research will follow an econometrics logical positivism tradition by using random-effects panel-data estimation on data derived from publicly available sources to test the hypothesis that entrepreneurial activity moderated by economic and personal freedoms cause positive economic well-being, specifically financial benefits on a subnational level, when controlling for other independent socio-economic variation between U.S. states. This empirical methodology best represents the data as constructs to reveal relationships between economic welfare, entrepreneurship, and economic freedom in support of theory (Hair, Black, Babin, Anderson, & Tatham, 2006).

The Theoretical Model

The basic theoretical model for empirical analysis is expressed, as follows:

$$LOG(REAL\_GSP_{jk}) = a_0 + a_1 STARTUP\_INDEX_{jk} + a_2 MAINSTREET\_INDEX_{jk}$$
$$+ a_3 GROWTH\_INDEX_{jk} + a_4 EFNA\_A3\_SUBN_{jk} + a_5 UNEMP\_RATE_{jk}$$
$$+ a_6 P\_BACH_{jk} + a_7 P\_HIGH\_ONLY_{jk} + \varepsilon_j \qquad (1)$$

The precise definitions of the variables in the semi-log specification described by Equation 1 are as follows:

$LOG(REAL\_GSP_{jk})$	The logarithm of Real Per Capita Gross State Product in State j in Year k
a_0	Constant
$STARTUP\_INDEX_{jk}$	KIEA Startup Index for State j in Year k
$MAINSTREET\_INDEX_{jk}$	KIEA Mainstreet Index for State j in Year k
$GROWTH\_INDEX_{jk}$	KIEA Growth Index for State j in Year k
$EFNA\_A3\_SUBN_{jk}$	The measure of Economic Freedom EFNA Subnational Component A3 Labor Freedom in State j in Year k
$UNEMP\_RATE_{jk}$	Average Annual Unemployment Rate in State j in Year k
P_BACH_{jk}	Percentage of Population with Bachelor's Degree or Higher in State j in Year k
$P\_HIGH\_ONLY_{jk}$	Percentage of Population with a High School Degree calculated as the Percentage of Population with a High School Degree or Equivalency in State j in Year k less the percentage of Population with a postsecondary degree.
ε_j	Stochastic Error Term

The secondary data was collected for the 50 states from 2008 through 2016 following the recession that started in late 2007. As discussed previously, this period offers a unique perspective on entrepreneurial activities and their antecedents and consequences in a broad jobless recovery suggestive of a systemic reduction in dynamism or structural change related to early form formation. The descriptive statistics are included in the Appendix in table A.1.

The second specification uses a log-log transformation and the explanatory variables are adjusted to facilitate log-log analysis. The empirical results including R^2 can be compared for the REAL_GSP dependent variable is the log-form in both equations (1) and (2).

$$LOG(REAL\_GSP_{jk}) = a_0 + a_1 LOG(LSTARTUP\_INDEX_{jk}) + a_2 LOG(LMAINSTREET\_INDEX_{jk}) + a_3$$
$$LOG(LGROWTH\_INDEX_{jk}) + a_4 LOG(EFNA\_A3\_SUBN_{jk}) + a_5 LOG(UNEMP\_RATE_{jk})$$
$$+ a_6 LOG(P\_BACH_{jk}) + a_7 LOG(P\_HIGH\_ONLY_{jk}) + \varepsilon_j \qquad (2)$$

The precise definitions of the variables in the modified log-log equation are, as follows:

$LOG(REAL\_GSP_{jk})$	The logarithm of Real Per Capita Gross State Product in State j in Year k
a_0	Constant
$LSTARTUP\_INDEX_{jk}$	KIEA Startup Index for State j in Year k offset by +5% to create a positive index for logarithmic estimation
$LMAINSTREET\_INDEX_{jk}$	KIEA Mainstreet Index for State j in Year k offset by +5% to create a positive index for logarithmic estimation
$LGROWTH\_INDEX_{jk}$	KIEA Growth Index for State j in Year k offset by +5% to create a positive index for logarithmic estimation
$EFNA\_A3\_SUBN_{jk}$	The measure of Economic Freedom EFNA Subnational Component A3 Labor Freedom in State j in Year k
$UNEMP\_RATE_{jk}$	Average Annual Unemployment Rate in State j in Year k
P_BACH_{jk}	Percentage of Population with Bachelor's Degree or Higher in State j in Year k
$P\_HIGH\_ONLY_{jk}$	Percentage of Population with a High School Degree calculated as the Percentage of Population with a High School Degree or Equivalency in State j in Year k less the percentage of Population with a postsecondary degree.
ε_j	Stochastic Error Term

For the log-log estimates, the KIEA indices have been adjusted by adding 5% to each indicator to make the subcomponents non-negative for log-log transformation, as LSTARTUP_INDEX, LMAINSTREET_INDEX, and LGROWTH_INDEX. The Personal Freedom index was also adapted for log-log comparison by adding one (+1) to the US50_PERSONAL indicator.

Linear panel equation estimation techniques for random effects were used in this study. A random-effects model approach was chosen based on the Hausman Test of the estimated correlation between the errors and the regressors in the proposed model (Hausman, 1978). The null hypothesis for the Hausman test assumes a minimal correlation between the error terms and the model regressors, whereby results using random effects will be validated. The alternate hypothesis suggests the preferred model is subject to fixed effect influences. The test criteria for the test is a 95% or greater probability of rejecting the Null hypothesis as determined by the p-value being less than or equal to 5% (0.05). The results of the Hausman Test are depicted in Table 3.4 in which the p-value of the null hypothesis is 7.31% and is greater than the test criteria of the p-value being less than 0.05.

Table 3.4 Hausman Test Results

Correlated Random Effects - Hausman Test			
Test Summary	Chi-Sq.	Prob.	Criteria
Cross-section random	12.958	7.31%	$p < 0.05$

Cross-section random effects test comparisons:				
Variable	Fixed	Random	Var. (Diff.)	Prob.
MAINSTREET_INDEX	0.0055	0.0078	0.0000	0.0678
STARTUP_INDEX	0.0027	0.0030	0.0000	0.3781
GROWTH_INDEX	0.0061	0.0063	0.0000	0.2390
EFNA_A3_SUBN	0.0671	0.0576	0.0000	0.0042
UNEMP_RATE	-0.0030	-0.0033	0.0000	0.3991
P_BACH	0.0015	0.0070	0.0000	0.0166
P_HIGH_ONLY	0.0077	0.0062	0.0000	0.4992

Therefore, the Null hypothesis is accepted, and the study will employ a random effects approach as appropriate. These Hausman specification test results can be further interpreted as a hypothesis-driven test for endogeneity as the coefficient is insignificant, the hypothesis of endogeneity can be rejected.

With the theoretical models defined and the variables in the models described, the analysis of the model and estimation calculations will proceed using IHS Inc.'s EVIEWS™ statistical software. The EVIEWS software will be used to compute panel equation estimates using linear general least squares (GLS) with correction for random effects. EVIEWS is the leading macroeconomic forecasting and analysis tool used by over 600 central banks and government institutions around the globe including the IMF, the World Bank and the United Nations (IHS, 2018). Academic researchers in over 1,600 universities and half of the Fortune's Top 100 Companies also use EVIEWS for econometric research (IHS, 2018).

The study's use of panel data presents advantages over ordinary time series or cross section (pooled) data with significant amounts of data. Panel data allows the study to control for unobservable influences that would degrade more traditional regression estimation approaches. The study will use data from 2008 to 2016 organized as 450 observations (50 X 9 panel dimensions) made up of 37,800 data points from 84 series. The central assumption for random effects estimation is that the random effects in this study's model are uncorrelated with the explanatory variables. This study's random effects specifications assume that the corresponding effects are independent random variables e.g. the random effects are uncorrelated with the residuals and have a mean of zero and finite variance. EVIEWS random effects models use a two-way random effects specification and the composite errors are estimated with the Wansbeek-Kapteyn method (Griliches, Engle, Intriligator, & McFadden, 1983). It should be noted that EVIEWS automatically adds constants to the common coefficients portion of the specification to ensure that the effects sum to zero (IHS, 2018). More detailed information on EVIEWS can be found on their website at www.eviews.com.

CHAPTER FOUR: FINDINGS

The objective of this investigation is to determine the financial benefits from specific entrepreneurial activities within a state while controlling for economic freedom and a variety of demographic and public policy variables. Based on the models described in this study, i.e., positive financial outcomes at the state level may be derived from the level of startup activity (STARTUP_INDEX), traditional business activity (MAINSTREET_INDEX), and established business growth (GROWTH_INDEX) mediated by labor freedom (EFNA_A3_SUBN) at the subnational level. Education attainment measured by P_BACH and P_HIGH_ONLY also contribute to positive financial outcomes at the state level. The estimates use the following empirical models;

Semi-log Model Specification:

$$
\begin{aligned}
\text{LOG(REAL\_GSP}jk) = {} & a_0 + a_1\text{MAINSTREET\_INDEX}\,jk + a_2\text{STARTUP\_INDEX}\,jk \\
& + a_3\ \text{GROWTH\_INDEX}jk + a_4\ \text{EFNA\_A3\_SUBN}jk + a_5\text{UNEMP\_RATE}jk \\
& + a_6\ \text{P\_BACH}jk + a_7\text{P\_HIGH\_ONLY}jk + \varepsilon j
\end{aligned}
\tag{3}
$$

Log-log Model Specification:

$$
\begin{aligned}
\text{LOG(REAL\_GSP}jk) = {} & a_0 + a_1\text{LOG(LMAINSTREET\_INDEX}jk) \\
& + a_2\text{LOG(LSTARTUP\_INDEX}jk) + a_3\ \text{LOG(LGROWTH\_INDEX}jk) \\
& + a_4\ \text{LOG(EFNA\_A3\_SUBN}jk) + a_5\ \text{LOG(UNEMP\_RATE}jk) \\
& + a_6\ \text{LOG(P\_BACH}jk) + a_7\ \text{LOG(P\_HIGH\_ONLY}jk) + \varepsilon j
\end{aligned}
\tag{4}
$$

where a_0 = constant term and ε is a stochastic error term. The coefficients in the above models are expected to have signs that positively or negatively impact state financial outcomes as follows:

$$a_1 > 0, \quad a_2 > 0, \quad a_3 > 0, \quad a_4 > 0, \quad a_5 < 0, \quad a_6 > 0, \quad a_7 > 0$$

Additionally, consistent results are expected using real median household income (RMED_HHINCOME) and per capita personal income (PCPERINCOME) as dependent variables and alternate measures of state financial outcomes. Freedom indices for economic labor freedom (EFNA_A3_SUBN) and personal freedom (US50_PERSONAL) are expected to have a positive and statistically significant influence on state-level financial outcomes related to the benefits of entrepreneurial pursuits.

Results

The semi-log estimation results of equation 3 are provided in Table 4.1, with estimated coefficients, t-values and probability values described. All the estimated coefficients on the explanatory variables exhibit the expected signs, and five of the seven coefficients are statistically significant. The explanatory variables MAINSTREET_INDEX, GROWTH_INDEX, EFNA_A3_SUBN, UNEMP_RATE, and P_BACH are significant at or beyond the 1% level. The explanatory variables for STARTUP and P_HIGH_ONLY have the correct signs but are not statistically significant at the 10% level. The semi-log model has an adjusted R^2 = 33.0% and an F-statistic of more than 29.0 (p-value = 0.0000), suggesting the model explains approximately one-third of the variation in state-level financial benefits actualized by REAL_GSP. Notably, early startup and new business formation defined by the level of new startup activity, STARTUP_INDEX, was not significant as hypothesized.

Table 4.1 Random Effects Semi-Log Results

Panel Estimation Results, Semi-log Entrepreneurial Financial Contribution 2008-2016

Dependent Variable: Real Gross State Product: LOG(REAL_GSP)

Variable	Coefficient	t-Statistic	Prob.	S.S.
MAINSTREET_INDEX	0.01578	3.2400	0.0013	***
STARTUP_INDEX	0.00307	1.3346	0.1828	
GROWTH_INDEX	0.00654	4.7564	0.0000	***
EFNA_A3_SUBN	0.07495	6.1152	0.0000	***
UNEMP_RATE	-0.01058	-4.2526	0.0000	***
P_BACH	0.01494	3.0458	0.0025	***
P_HIGH_ONLY	0.00564	1.2858	0.1993	
C	9.52400	24.8238	0.0000	

***S.S. at the 1% level; ** S.S. at the 5% level; *S.S. at the 10% level

***statistically significant (S.S) at the 1% level; ** S.S. at the 5% level; *S.S. at the 10% level

R-squared	34.20%
Adjusted R-squared	33.02%
F-statistic	29.105***
Prob. (F-statistic)	0.0000

The Random Effects estimation results for the log-log specification of the model in equation 4 are provided in Table 4.2, where estimated coefficients, t-values, and p-value probabilities are listed. All seven explanatory variables display coefficients with the expected signs, and five of the seven coefficients are statistically significant. Four of explanatory variables, MAINSTREET_INDEX, GROWTH_INDEX, EFNA_A3_SUBN, and UNEMP_RATE, are statistically significant at or beyond the 1% level. The significance of the MAINSTREET_INDEX explanatory variable increased over the previous semi-log model, while higher education achievement defined by P_BACH was statistically significant at the 5% level. The explanatory variables for STARTUP_INDEX and P_HIGH_ONLY had the expected sings but were not statistically significant at the 10% level. The log-log model has an adjusted $R^2 = $ 32.9% and an F-statistic of 29.0, suggesting this model also explains a third of the variation in financial benefits from entrepreneurial activities at the state level. Again, early startup and new business formation activities described by the STARTUP_INDEX were not statistically

significant. Both the semi-log and log-log models produced consistent empirical results.

Table 4.2 Random Effects Log-log Results

Panel Estimation Results, Entrepreneurial Log-Log Financial Contribution 2008-2016
Dependent Variable: Real Gross State Product: LOG(REAL_GSP)

Variable	Coefficient	t-statistic	Prob.	S.S.
LOG(LMAINSTREET_INDEX)	0.09565	4.70246	0.0000	***
LOG(LSTARTUP_INDEX)	0.00683	0.74496	0.4567	
LOG(LGROWTH)	0.02871	4.68601	0.0000	***
LOG(EFNA_A3_SUBN)	0.45130	5.44526	0.0000	***
LOG(UNEMP_RATE)	-0.12393	-6.42859	0.0000	***
LOG(P_BACH)	0.25897	2.23012	0.0263	**
LOG(P_HIGH_ONLY)	0.11638	0.52642	0.5989	
C	8.54749	7.34402	0.0000	

***S.S. at the 1% level; ** S.S. at the 5% level; *S.S. at the 10% level

R-squared	34.12%
Adjusted R-squared	32.94%
F-statistic	29.00***
Prob. (F-statistic)	0.0000

Hypotheses

The empirical results suggest entrepreneurial activities described by the KIEA

subcomponents and EFNA exhibit a positive and statistically significant impact on real per capita

gross state product when controlling for human capital and labor market influences, as

hypothesized. The results illustrate and largely support the main hypotheses as described below.

H1: Startup activity will have a positive and statistically significant effect on

REAL_GSP, *ceteris paribus.* The results fail to accept this hypothesis because the relationship

between the startup activity index and real per capita state product is positive but not statistically

significant. Increasing the rate of new entrepreneurs within a state may not create additional

financial benefits or may take more than a decade to manifest.

H2: Mainstreet Activity will have a positive and statistically significant effect on

REAL_GSP, *ceteris paribus.* At the 1% statistical significance level, the hypothesis is accepted. Main street business activity within the state has a positive economic impact and produces financial benefits at the state-level. Increasing local business ownership, survival rates, and the prevalence of local small businesses may have a positive impact on state GSP.

H3: Growth Activity will have a positive and statistically significant effect on REAL_GSP, *ceteris paribus.* At the 1% statistical significance level, the hypothesis is accepted, with entrepreneurial growth within a state having a positive economic impact and producing financial benefits at the state-level. This finding suggests that more fast-growing and high-growth entrepreneurial businesses increase financial benefit at the state level.

The KIEA indices and subcomponent indices are found to be useful indicators of entrepreneurial activity, but the composite indices are difficult to equate with specific actionable and tractable guidance for researchers, practitioners, and local and state policy makers. The explanatory variables used in this study are normalized indicators from the KIEA and EFNA state-level indices, and these indicators may be further decomposed into their constituent parts, which may provide additional clarity and insights. To this end, the statistically significant explanatory variables in equation 4 are further decomposed and analyzed using a step-wise approach to construct a model using the lowest level of KIEA components. The results of this empirical decomposition are displayed in Table 4.3, where estimated coefficients, t-values and probabilities of sub-component constituents are provided. The decomposition selects constituent parts of the MAINSTREET_INDEX, GROWTH_INDEX and EFNA subcomponents, which are highly correlated with the explanatory variables exhibiting the expected signs and statistical significance in accordance with the theoretical model(s) previously described.

Table 4.3 Indicator Decomposition

Panel Estimation Results, KIEA & EFNA Subcomponent Decomposition 2008-2016

Dependent Variable: Real Gross State Product: LOG(REAL_GSP)

Variable	Coefficient	t-Statistic	Prob.	S.S.
MSURVIVAL_RATE	0.30276	4.0269	0.0001	***
GSTART_GROWTH	0.01540	1.7437	0.0820	*
GSHARE_SCALE	3.36042	2.7979	0.0054	***
UNEMP_RATE	-0.00239	-1.4118	0.1588	
EFNA_3Ai_SUBN	0.03959	6.1570	0.0000	***
EFNA_3Aii_SUBN	0.00942	1.7143	0.0873	*
P_BACH	0.01058	3.5609	0.0004	***
P_HIGHSCHL	0.00702	1.9784	0.0486	**
C	9.27158	33.4686	0.0000	

***S.S. at the 1% level; ** S.S. at the 5% level; *S.S. at the 10% level

R-squared	0.405692
Adjusted R-squared	0.393532
F-statistic	33.36***
Prob. (F-statistic)	0

The KIEA subcomponents are further decomposed into their underlying constituent subparts to gain additional understanding using MSURVIVAL_RATE (for MAINSTREET_INDEX), SHARE_SCALE (for GROWTH_INDEX), GSTART_GROWTH (for GROWTH_INDEX) and EFNA_3Ai_SUBN and EFNA_3Aii_SUBN (for EFNA_A3_SUBN) as explanatory variables. The coefficients on MSURVIVAL_RATE, SHARE_SCALE, and EFNA_3Ai_SUBN are found to be positive and significant at the 1% level. The GSTART_GROWTH and EFNA_3Aii_SUBN are positive and significant at the 10% level. Educational achievement defined by P_BACH and P_HIGH_ONLY are positive and significant at the 1% and 5% levels, respectively. This "bottom-up" empirical model has an adjusted R^2 = 39% and an F-statistic of 33.0, which has slightly better explanatory power and statistical significance than the study's previous results for equation 4.

These findings suggest that entrepreneurial businesses that grow to become a medium-sized business with 50 or more employees over a 10-year timeframe have a significant impact at the state level. These results further suggest that main street entrepreneurship driven predominately by increasing business survival rates has a significant and positive financial benefit at the state-level. The results also suggest financial benefits are not derived from early startup activities, but from sustaining startup growth rates for at least five years. The results also confirm that the prevalence of fast-growing, private companies with at least 20% annualized growth over three years contribute significantly to the state economy. The results in Table 4.3 highlight EFNA_3Ai_SUBN as more significant at the 1% level with a coefficient that is an order of magnitude greater than EFNA_3Aii_SUBN, which is only significant at the 10% level. This suggests the influence of the minimum wage indicator (EFNA_3Ai_SUBN) is more significant and has a greater influence on financial outcomes than relative differences in state employment levels (EFNA_3Aii_SUBN).

H4: Economic Freedom has a positive and statistically significant effect on REAL_GSP, *ceteris paribus*. At the 1% statistical significance level, the hypothesis is accepted, and the EFNA Area 3 subnational component has a positive influence on entrepreneurial activity and significant impact on financial benefits at the state-level. This finding suggests that increasing labor freedom and promoting an entrepreneurial environment has profound financial benefits for states. Policies that increase private enterprise, reduce government size (employment), and eliminate "red-tape" regulations on small business and entrepreneurial activities will have a positive financial impact at the state-level. Removing restrictions on new entrants to the workforce, encouraging productivity and promoting right-to-work law(s) may have a significant influence on positive financial outcomes at the state level. The findings also suggest that understanding the influences of the EFNA sub-components may be more important

40

than the overall freedom index at the state and local level, *ceteris paribus*.

Multiple indices and measures of freedom were considered for this study, with EFNA used as the primary explanatory indicator of institutional quality. Prior research has found EFW, EFNA and US50 Indices to be relevant and contributory. This study highlights some important observations and challenges of incorporating "freedoms" related to financial outcomes and entrepreneurial influences at the state level. Empirical estimates using the individual EFNA subcomponents along with the respective coefficients, t-values and p-value probabilities are summarized in Table 4.4. The EFNA area subcomponents exhibited diverse effects on the results with EFNA_A2_SUBN suggesting a statistically significant but negative influence and EFNA_A1_SUBN not being statistically significant. The overall aggregate EFNA subnational indicator (EFNA_OVERALL_SUBN) was not found to be statistically significant. The EFNA_A3_SUBN indicator was found to be statistically significant and positive in all cases.

Table 4.4 EFNA Subnational Estimates

Variable	Coefficient	t-Statistic	Prob.	S.S.
LOG(EFNA_A1_SUBN)	-0.03073	-0.828053	0.4081	
LOG(EFNA_A2_SUBN)	-0.18461	-3.349316	0.0009	***
LOG(EFNA_A3_SUBN)	0.451299	5.44526	0.0000	***
LOG(EFNA_OVERALL_SUBN)	-0.05151	-0.604236	0.5460	
***S.S. at the 1% level; ** S.S. at the 5% level; *S.S. at the 10% level				

The correlation matrix for the Economic Freedom indicators including EFNA and its respective subcomponents are described in Table A.3 in the Appendix. For the subnational EFNA indices, the overall economic freedom index (EFNA_OVERALL_SUBN) highly correlates with all three sub-component area indicators, EFNA_A1_SUBN, EFNA_A2_SUBN, and EFNA_A3_SUBN. EFNA_A3_SUBN is the most statistically significant below the 1% level and is approximately three times more influential than any other EFNA subnational component when assessed individually. This comparison suggests that overall economic freedom at the subnational level is not a significant differentiator between states in terms of entrepreneurship. Likewise, taxation indicated by EFNA_A2_SUBN exhibits a negative influence on financial benefits indicative of "unproductive" entrepreneurial opportunities not encompassed by the KIEA indicators. Labor freedom indicated by EFNA_A3_SUBN is positive and statistically significant, which supports its use as a proxy for economic freedom influences on productive entrepreneurial activities at the subnational level. Therefore, EFNA_A3_SUBN is found to be the preferred indicator of economic freedom at the state level, highlighting the contribution of the relevant economic freedom(s) to entrepreneurship as defined in this study.

The Ruger & Sorens freedom indices offer the addition of personal freedom, which was treated as an extension to the EFNA subnational considerations. The US50 indices for economic freedom (US50_ECONOMIC), it's component parts, US50_FISCAL and US50_REGULATORY, were found to be statistically significant and negative when incorporated into the model. EFNA was chosen in lieu of the US50 indices because the US50 data is published every other year and decreases the sample size by 50%. Inferences from empirical estimates become fragile if the sample size is too small. Additionally, the US50 indices were found to be statistically significant but may interact with the dependent and explanatory variables because of being normalized with GDP. By contrast, EFNA uses PERINCOME.

The study estimates the influence of personal freedom for (US50_PERSONAL) as an extension of EFNA economic freedom. The results of a confirmatory empirical analysis adapting US50_PERSONAL as an additional explanatory variable for log-log analysis are depicted in Table 4.7. Consistent with this study's primary findings, MAINSTREET_INDEX, GROWTH_INDEX, EFNA_A3_SUBN, P_BACH and UNEMP_RATE retain the correct sign and are statistically significant.

Table 4.7 Ancillary Test Results

Panel Estimation Results, Addition of Personal Freedom 2008-2016

Dependent Variable: Real Gross State Product: LOG(REAL_GSP)

Variable	Coefficient	t-Statistic	Prob.	S.S.
LOG(LMAINSTREET_INDEX)	0.05258	2.30071	0.02230	**
LOG(LSTARTUP_INDEX)	0.00687	0.53439	0.59360	
LOG(LGROWTH)	0.03797	4.68352	0.00000	***
LOG(EFNA_A3_SUBN)	0.27551	2.68938	0.00770	***
LOG(US50_PERSONAL+1)	0.02026	0.24080	0.80990	
LOG(UNEMP_RATE)	-0.03235	-2.35485	0.01930	**
LOG(P_BACH)	0.32216	3.25040	0.00130	***
LOG(P_HIGH_ONLY)	-0.05195	-0.20580	0.83710	
C	9.24984	7.65042	0.00000	

***statistically significant (S.S) at the 1% level; ** S.S. at the 5% level; *S.S. at the 10% level

R-squared	32.83%
Adjusted R-squared	30.60%
F-statistic	14.722***
Prob. (F-statistic)	0.00000

The estimated coefficient and the personal freedom variable (US50_PERSONAL) is not statistically significant and does not exhibit significant influence on entrepreneurial-related financial benefits at the state level, which is also confirmatory based on prior research (Hafer, 2013; Hall et al., 2013). Again, explanatory variables for STARTUP_INDEX and P_HIGH_ONLY have the expected sign but are not statistically significant. The model in Table 4.6 has an adjusted R2 of 30.6% and an F-statistic of 14.7, which is also consistent with the study's primary result(s). Personal freedom (US50_PERSONAL) was neither statistically significant nor useful with respect to explaining state-level financial benefits and entrepreneurship.

In summary, decomposing EFNA economic freedom and augmenting area freedoms with personal freedom suggests findings at the subnational level related to hypothesis H4 as follows;

H4A: GOVERNMENT SPENDING does not have a statistically significant effect at the subnational level, *ceteris paribus*

H4B: TAX FREEDOM has a negative and statistically significant effect at the subnational level, *ceteris paribus*

H4C: LABOR FREEDOM has a positive and statistically significant effect, *ceteris paribus*

H4D: US50_PERSONAL does not have statistically significant effect at the subnational level, *ceteris paribus*

Labor Freedom defined by EFNA_A3_SUBN has the most significant and positive effect on entrepreneurial-economic outcomes. State tax impacts are statistically significant and exhibit a negative influence on entrepreneurial economic outcomes, which is consistent with prior work (Krichevskiy & Snyder, 2015). Taxation at the subnational level is subsumed by federal tax influences and considered minor in comparison to labor freedom influences on the subnational level. The aggregate-level of economic freedom on a subnational level and the variation in personal freedom defined by US50_PERSONAL do not exhibit any significant influence on REAL_GSP at the state level, which is also consistent with prior research (Campbell et al., 2013a; Hafer, 2013).

Ancillary Test Results

This study's empirical findings are related to ancillary research questions to confirm consistency with earlier studies from which the ancillary hypotheses were formed. Ancillary test results for the UNEMP, P_BACH and P_HIGH_ONLY control variables are consistent with prior work as discussed below.

Ha: UNEMP_RATE has a negative and statistically significant effect, *ceteris paribus*.
At the 1% statistical significance level, the real per capita gross state product is inversely related to the state-level unemployment rate. This finding suggests declining unemployment at the state-level increases entrepreneurial activity and financial benefits. This finding may also suggest that entrepreneurship is being driven by opportunity rather than necessity at the state level.

Hb: P_BACH has a positive and statistically significant effect, *ceteris paribus*.
At the 1% statistical significance level in the semi-log model and at the 5% statistical significance level in the log-log model, real per capita gross state product is positively related to the percentage of a state's population with a bachelor's degree. This finding suggests that the higher education attainments in a state, the better the state-level financial outcomes. Increasing post-secondary graduation rates as well as recruiting and retaining a college-educated workforce within the state promotes increased entrepreneurial activity and greater economic prosperity.

Hc: P_HIGH_ONLY has a positive and statistically significant effect, *ceteris paribus*.
The percentage of adults attaining only a high school degree or equivalency within the state did not exhibit a statistically significant influence on entrepreneurial outcomes, although this indicator exhibited the expected, positive sign. The real per capita gross state product is not influenced by the variation in the percentage of a state's population who attain a high school education.

State-level Per Capita Personal Income (PCPERINCOME) and Real Median Household Income (RMED_HHINCOME) are assessed as alternative measures of financial benefits at the subnational for confirmatory empirical analysis. The results of this ancillary analysis using PCPERINCOME in place of REAL_GSP in equation (4) are confirmatory and depicted in Table 4.5, which includes estimated coefficients, t-values, and p-value probabilities. The explanatory variables, MAINSTREET_INDEX, GROWTH_INDEX, EFNA_A3_SUBN, P_BACH and UNEMP_RATE, exhibit the expected sign and are statistically significant at or below the 1% level when using PCPERINCOME as the alternate dependent variable.

Table 4.5 Ancillary Results

Panel Estimation Results, Log-Log Financial Contribution 2008-2016
Dependent Variable: LOG(PCPERINCOME)

Variable	Coefficient	t-Statistic	Prob.	S.S.
LOG(LMAINSTREET_INDEX)	0.04506	3.2026	0.0015	***
LOG(LSTARTUP_INDEX)	-0.00063	-0.0982	0.9218	
LOG(LGROWTH)	0.01776	4.1542	0.0000	***
LOG(EFNA_A3_SUBN)	0.33389	5.8482	0.0000	***
LOG(P_BACH)	0.22128	2.9285	0.0036	***
LOG(P_HIGH_ONLY)	-0.21387	-1.4488	0.1482	
LOG(UNEMP_RATE)	-0.09244	-6.9173	0.0000	***
C	10.20368	13.0997	0.0000	
***S.S. at the 1% level; ** S.S. at the 5% level; *S.S. at the 10% level				
R-squared	0.245838			
Adjusted R-squared	0.232371			
F-statistic	18.254***			
Prob. (F-statistic)	0.0000			

Also consistent with this study's primary results, the explanatory variables for STARTUP_INDEX and P_HIGH_ONLY are not statistically significant. The estimate for PCPERINCOME has an adjusted R^2 of 24.5% and an F-statistic of 18.2, which are consistent with our previous findings for REAL_GSP and further confirm a relationship between financial benefits, entrepreneurial activity and economic freedom at the state level.

Table 4.6 Additional Ancillary Results

Panel Estimation Results, Log-Log Financial Contribution 2008-2016

Dependent Variable: LOG(RMED_HHINCOME)

Variable	Coefficient	t-Statistic	Prob.	S.S.
LOG(LMAINSTREET_INDEX)	0.06565	3.1163	0.0020	***
LOG(LSTARTUP_INDEX)	0.00838	0.6470	0.5180	
LOG(LGROWTH)	0.03574	4.0792	0.0001	***
LOG(EFNA_A3_SUBN)	-0.31462	-3.4334	0.0007	***
LOG(P_BACH)	0.47829	6.4281	0.0000	***
LOG(P_HIGH_ONLY)	-0.14668	-0.8160	0.4150	
LOG(UNEMP_RATE)	-0.07078	-4.8892	0.0000	***
C	10.47975	11.2453	0.0000	

***S.S. at the 1% level; ** S.S. at the 5% level; *S.S. at the 10% level

R-squared	0.167792
Adjusted R-squared	0.150764
F-statistic	9.85***
Prob. (F-statistic)	0.0000

Similarly, Real Median Household Income (RMED_HHINCOME) is used as an alternative measure of financial benefits at the state-level based on equation (4). The empirical results when using RMED_HHINCOME as the dependent variable in place of REAL_GSP are consistent as described in Table 4.6, with estimated coefficients, t-values and p-value probabilities. Again, the explanatory variables; MAINSTREET_INDEX, GROWTH_INDEX, P_BACH, and UNEMP_RATE are confirmed to have the correct sign and statistical significance at or below the 1% level. EFNA_A3_SUBN is significant but exhibits a negative influence on real median household income. Again, the variables for STARTUP_INDEX and P_HIGH_ONLY are not statistically significant. The ancillary model has an R^2 and an F-statistic lower than all previous estimates. The overall results using RMED_HHINCOME as the alternate dependent variable are consistent with previous findings and suggest increased labor freedom at the state level may have a negative influence on real median household incomes.

Multicolinearity Tests

Several statistical and confirmatory tests are performed to endeavor to support the findings and confirm the robustness of the model(s) and indicators used in this study. These tests are intended to address common issues in econometrics analysis and modeling including collinearity, multicollinearity, and structural validity. The descriptive statistics for the variables and related secondary data used in this study are listed in Table A.1 in the appendices. Both skewness and kurtosis are described for comparison of the variables' statistical distribution shape to a normal distribution. Note: a skewness of 0 and kurtosis of 3 characterizes a normal distribution.

A major concern with decomposing the KIEA indices is the potential problem of multicollinearity between the index subcomponents because they are usually closely related. To assess possible multicollinearity problems among the three KIEA subcomponents, variance inflation factors (VIF) are used to quantify how much the estimated regression coefficients are inflated. The VIF test is readily accomplished with EVIEWS, and results for both the semi-log and the log-log equations used in this study are depicted in Table 4.8

The rule of thumb is that VIFs exceeding five warrant further investigation, while VIFs exceeding ten are signs of serious multicollinearity requiring correction (IHS, 2018). Surveying the VIF results in Table 4.8 shows the explanatory variables used in both the semi-log model (Equation 3) and the log-log model (Equation 4) do not exhibit any significant multicollinearity issues. The VIF values for the explanatory variables vary between 1.2 and 3.3 for the semi-log equation, which are below our threshold of concern near 5. Likewise, the VIF values for the explanatory variables vary between 1.02 and 1.52 for the log-log equation, which are also below our threshold of concern. Therefore, the findings in this study are not subject to multicollinearity concerns based on the variance inflation factor results.

Table 4.8 Variance Inflation Factor (VIF) Test Results

VIF Analysis for Semi-Log Equation 3

Semi-log Variables	Coefficient VAR	VIF
MAINSTREET_INDEX	1.46E-05	1.6017
STARTUP_INDEX	5.33E-06	1.6449
GROWTH_INDEX	1.71E-06	1.2645
EFNA_A3_SUBN	0.000115	2.9207
UNEMP_RATE	2.29E-06	2.2913
P_BACH	1.08E-05	3.2931
P_HIGHSCHL	1.44E-05	2.8780
C	0.077586	NA

VIF Analysis for Log-Log Equation 4

Log-Log Variables	Coefficient VAR	VIF
LOG(LMAINSTREET_INDEX)	4.14E-04	1.051943
LOG(LSTARTUP_INDEX)	8.42E-05	1.045468
LOG(LGROWTH)	3.75E-05	1.021386
LOG(EFNA_A3_SUBN)	0.006869	1.019774
LOG(UNEMP_RATE)	3.72E-04	1.036373
LOG(P_BACH)	1.35E-02	1.453898
LOG(P_HIGH_ONLY)	4.89E-02	1.439692
C	1.354596	NA

The correlation matrix the Kauffman Index of Entrepreneurial Activity and its subcomponents and their constituent parts are listed in table A.3 in the Appendix. Surveying these results for the KIEA indices finds no significant linear association between explanatory variables related to the findings. There is a very low correlation between the KIEA Growth, Mainstreet and Startup indices, confirming the independence and uniqueness for each of the indicators used in this study. Additionally, there is no significant linear association between the KIEA indices and the other the explanatory variables. The MAINSTREET_INDEX highly correlates with two of its three constituent parts; the business survival rate (MSURVIVAL_RATE) and the rate of sole proprietorships (MRATE_OF_BUSINESS_OWNERS). The KIEA Growth Index highly correlates with all three of its subcomponents parts.

Subsequent robustness tests on the EFNA subnational indices find only the EFNA_A2_SUBN and EFNA_A3_SUBN indicators to be statistically significant in this study. A comparison between the EFNA indices and US50 freedom indices finds significant correlation between EFNA_A2_SUBN and the US50 components. The personal freedom indicator (US50_PERSONAL) does not significantly correlate with any other EFNA or US50 variables used in this study's estimates. Using EFNA_A3_SUBN as the primary indicator of economic freedom, the study is not subject to any significant linear associations between the explanatory variables. As such, multicollinearity issues are not a significant concern for the findings in this study.

Robustness Tests

To examine structural validity or uncertainty of the models, several robustness checks are conducted. Econometric empirical studies commonly examine "robustness" by analyzing how regression coefficient estimates of the "core" explanatory variables behave when the regression specification is modified by adding and removing regressors (Lu & White, 2014). The core variables in the log-log model include the KIEA subcomponents, LMAINSTREET_INDEX, LSTARTUP_INDEX, and LGROWTH_INDEX and the EFNA subcomponent, EFNA_A3_SUBN. The remaining control variables, P_BACH, P_HIGH_ONLY, and UNEMP, are removed individually. The robustness test results for removing individual control variables are shown in Table 4.9.

Table 4.9 Robustness Test Removing Regressors

Model/Test	Coefficient	t-statistic	Probability	R^2	Adj R^2	F-Stat	Prob. (F-Stat)
P_HIGH_ONLY removed							
LOG(LMAINSTREET_INDEX)	0.05021	2.97013	0.00320				
LOG(LSTARTUP_INDEX)	0.00524	0.55213	0.58120	33.97%	32.96%	33.696	0.00000
LOG(LGROWTH)	0.02668	4.34370	0.00000				
LOG(EFNA_A3_SUBN)	0.34117	4.51440	0.00000				
P_BACH Removed							
LOG(LMAINSTREET_INDEX)	0.03213	1.94733	0.05220				
LOG(LSTARTUP_INDEX)	-0.00200	-0.21257	0.83180	31.72%	30.68%	30.432	0.00000
LOG(LGROWTH)	0.02516	4.07134	0.00010				
LOG(EFNA_A3_SUBN)	0.46157	6.54800	0.00000				
UNEMP_RATE Removed							
LOG(LMAINSTREET_INDEX)	0.06237	3.73803	0.00020				
LOG(LSTARTUP_INDEX)	0.00517	0.53950	0.58980	32.68%	31.65%	31.799	0.00000
LOG(LGROWTH)	0.02597	4.19519	0.00000				
LOG(EFNA_A3_SUBN)	0.48099	8.35522	0.00000				

The core explanatory variables behave consistently with the previous findings, with LMAINSTREET_INDEX, LGROWTH_INDEX and, EFNA_A3_SUBN remaining statistically significant with similar coefficient values. LSTARTUP is never significant. The adjusted R^2

varies by no more than 10% from the original model with a consistent p-value = 0.00000.

The robustness testing is expanded by adding additional control variables based on prior works, which are individually added in the model for re-estimation. These regressors were chosen to ensure that robustness checks consist of; JAN_TEMP, ADV_DEGREES, IMMG_SHARE, NET_MIGR, PER_IMMG. The robustness test results for adding additional regressors are depicted in Table 4.10. Table 4.10 reveals consistent values for the significant explanatory variable coefficients, t-statistics, probabilities as well as overall adjusted R^2 and R^2 values and F-statistics in the majority of the tests.

Table 4.10 Robustness Tests Adding Regressors

Model/Test	Coefficient	t-statistic	Probability	R^2	Adj R^2	F-Stat	Prob. (F-Stat)
Add JAN_TEMP							
LOG(LMAINSTREET_INDEX)	0.05118	3.00822	0.00280				
LOG(LSTARTUP_INDEX)	0.00535	0.56212	0.57440	34.12%	32.77%	25.315	0.00000
LOG(LGROWTH)	0.02682	4.35381	0.00000				
LOG(EFNA_A3_SUBN)	0.33519	4.37153	0.00000				
Add ADV_DEGREES							
LOG(LMAINSTREET_INDEX)	0.05962	3.51260	0.00050				
LOG(LSTARTUP_INDEX)	0.00508	0.54283	0.58760	35.80%	34.49%	27.257	0.00000
LOG(LGROWTH)	0.02380	3.88141	0.00010				
LOG(EFNA_A3_SUBN)	0.30915	4.08015	0.00010				
Add IMMG_SHARE (%State Pop Immigrants)							
LOG(LMAINSTREET_INDEX)	0.05918	3.55220	0.00040				
LOG(LSTARTUP_INDEX)	0.00601	0.64982	0.51620	37.38%	36.09%	29.170	0.00000
LOG(LGROWTH)	0.02628	4.39562	0.00000				
LOG(EFNA_A3_SUBN)	0.32692	4.39295	0.00000				
Add PER_IMMG (Annual %change in state pop from immigration +1)							
LOG(LMAINSTREET_INDEX)	0.05019	2.83856	0.00480				
LOG(LSTARTUP_INDEX)	0.00171	0.17159	0.86390	29.14%	27.48%	17.531	0.00000
LOG(LGROWTH)	0.02919	4.56435	0.00000				
LOG(EFNA_A3_SUBN)	0.27938	3.34922	0.00090				
Add PER_NET_MIGR (Annual %Net Migration in/out State +1)							
LOG(LMAINSTREET_INDEX)	0.05150	3.02955	0.00260				
LOG(LSTARTUP_INDEX)	0.00542	0.57073	0.56850	34.15%	32.80%	25.349	0.00000
LOG(LGROWTH)	0.02668	4.32861	0.00000				
LOG(EFNA_A3_SUBN)	0.33639	4.39901	0.00000				

Lastly, the model was tested with sample data that excluded the states of Hawaii and Alaska as their economic inputs and outputs can be significantly different from the 48 contiguous states. Equation 4 was re-estimated after reducing the sample to the 48 contiguous states. The results of the empirical estimates sans Hawaii and Alaska are depicted in Table 4.11. These results also show consistent values for the explanatory variables coefficients, t-statistics, and probabilities for the core explanatory variables. This model has a consistent although slightly improved adjusted R^2 at 36%, as compared to ~33% in the original findings, which is consistent with the study's expectations for the reduced sample size.

Table 4.11 Robustness Test without Variables, AK and HI

Model/Test	Coefficient	t-statistic	Probability	R^2	Adj R^2	F-Stat	Prob. (F-Stat)
Sample: 2008 2016 IF STATENAME<>"Alaska" AND STATENAME<>"Hawaii							
LOG(LMAINSTREET_INDEX)	0.058835	3.491246	0.00050				
LOG(LSTARTUP_INDEX)	0.005798	0.605789	0.54500	37.21%	36.05%	31.838	0.00000
LOG(LGROWTH)	0.031094	4.909523	0.00000				
LOG(EFNA_A3_SUBN)	0.350183	4.603983	0.00000				

The robustness tests provide consistent and similar results for removing control variables, adding additional explanatory and control variables, and adjusting the sample to exclude potential economic disparity from Alaska and Hawaii. Consistent and robust coefficients can be interpreted as evidence of specification validity, and these additional diagnostics confirm robustness and further validate the findings in this study.

CHAPTER FIVE: CONCLUSIONS

Summary

The research question for this study is to empirically assess the impacts of prominent entrepreneurial activities and their interaction with economic and personal freedoms on economic welfare within the United States. This is the first study to decompose and combine the KIEA, EFNA and Personal Freedom indices in the context of declining U.S. entrepreneurial dynamism. The models and results herein define the dynamic nature of entrepreneurial activities and their relationship to positive state financial outcomes as measured by real per capita gross state product, per capita personal income and real median household income. The study finds the 2017 Kauffman Index of Entrepreneurial Activity indices for Startup Activity, Mainstreet Activity and High-Growth Business have advantages in explaining entrepreneurship, adding a more granular level of understanding to the body of prior work (Bjørnskov & Foss, 2016; Hall & Lawson, 2014). The KIEA indices are found to be robust and novel indicators of entrepreneurial activity at the state level.

The findings suggest increased entrepreneurial activity within a state has a direct influence on financial outcomes, more specifically improving per capita real gross state product and per capita personal income. Entrepreneurial activity explains over 32% of the variation in real gross state product at the state level and increasing labor freedom within a state has profound financial benefits. This study suggests states can benefit by helping entrepreneurial and local businesses both survive and thrive over multiple years. The study also suggests that isolated efforts to increase the number of startups and new businesses produce little additional benefit on their own. Neither the aggregate-level of economic freedom nor variation in personal freedom has a significant impact on state financial outcomes on the subnational level, which is also consistent with prior research (Campbell et al., 2013a; Hafer, 2013).

Discussion

The extant literature supports that claim that entrepreneurship creates wealth for individuals as well as economic well-being in the developed world, and economic freedom and institutional quality significantly influence these activities. Since 2008, the U.S. has experienced an accelerating decline in new business dynamism and entrepreneurial activity (Burger & Schwartz, 2018). At the same time, the U.S. economy has recovered from the great recession of 2008, and unemployment is now at the lowest level in over 40 years (Worstall, 2018). What isn't clear is which type of entrepreneurial activities and institutional policies promote positive financial outcomes under these economic conditions. The findings in this study suggest it may not be the quantity but the type of sustained entrepreneurial activity that is most important. More specifically, the research identifies specific types of entrepreneurial activities that "exploit" opportunities and positively affect U.S. State economies. The study is consistent with Baumol's concept of productive entrepreneurship (Baumol, 1990) and extends productive entrepreneurship as a more granular set of entrepreneurial activities that influence financial outcomes.

The findings suggest that merely increasing the rate of new entrepreneurs within a state does not create significant financial benefits. Likewise, the rate at which new businesses with employees are created is not a significant contributor to improving economic prosperity at the state level. Financial benefits are derived from the startup growth rate, which requires a longer-term commitment to sustaining growth for five years or longer. Additionally, increasing fast growing and high-growth entrepreneurial businesses creates financial benefits within the state. Seemingly straightforward, the prevalence of fast-growing, private companies with at least 20% annual growth for three years is highly beneficial to U.S. state economies. However, the KIEA Growth Index encompasses more than what we typically think of as high-tech "unicorns," suggesting state benefits are derived from achieving and sustaining the growth of both early-stage private companies as well as established businesses in multiple industries (Russell et al., 2017). Scaling high-growth entrepreneurial businesses is rare with less than 2% of early-stage businesses sustaining high growth for multiple years, so understanding the high-growth phenomenon in greater detail is highly recommended. The statistical significance and contribution of the main street activities may present the most undervalued opportunity to positively affect state financial outcomes. The findings suggest increasing local business ownership and survival rates will have a positive and significant impact on state economies.

Additional findings suggest that economic freedoms including minimum wage flexibility, government employment restraints, and right-to-work policies are the most significant factors that moderate positive entrepreneurial activities and their resulting financial benefits. Indicators for overall economic freedom are not statistically significant at the subnational level, which suggests the influence from the aggregate level of economic freedom on financial outcomes is muted at the state level. Higher education and undergraduate graduation rates fuel entrepreneurial activity and drive greater economic prosperity at the state level. The overall findings justify additional research and study into the complex entrepreneurial-institutional–economic trinity.

Implications

The study suggests that the broad decline in dynamism in the United States as measured by net job creation from startup businesses may not be a significant a cause for alarm. The findings suggest increasing main street activity and achieving higher growth of established businesses is what drives the financial benefits we desire as a nation, at least at the state level. These implications offer guidance and, perhaps, a word of caution and possible course correction for our business leaders, government officials, and academic institutions. This study endorses sustaining nascent and early-stage entrepreneurial activity as a prerequisite for economic prosperity but suggests re-prioritization on higher-value entrepreneurial activities that directly and significantly create produce positive economic outcomes. We need to look beyond early startup activity and the number of lone entrepreneurs as primary indicators of success. The study recommends longer-term assistance to increase the survival rates of main street businesses and foster a more capable workforce to power high-growth business success. Pro-entrepreneurial policies should promote small business development skills and sustainability for innovators and first movers (Parker & Parker, 2009).

The findings also suggest our national obsession and priority on startups and highly successful entrepreneurs may be misleading and counterproductive. Entrepreneurship is significantly biased by hindsight and inferring best practices and policies from "celebrity" entrepreneurs is like *studying gamblers by exclusively studying winners*" (Parker & Parker, 2009). Our popular culture's daily attention to celebrity entrepreneurs and the market's exuberance for unicorn businesses are filtering into our boardrooms and universities. This mindset is luring profitable and enduring corporations to pursue blue-sky ideas and hockey-stick disruption for growth, but growth should not come at the expense of foundational, established, business practices of balancing growth with return on invested capital (Lepore, 2018).

Policies and priorities focused solely on the early origins of entrepreneurship, specifically creating new businesses and increasing local startup density may not produce greater financial benefit in the United States. The presence of high-growth young firms highly skews firm growth rates, and this trend overemphasizes the contribution from new firms (Decker, Haltiwanger, Jarmin, & Miranda, 2016b). To that end, organizations and institutions must pursue policies and regulation (or lack thereof) that patiently encourage entrepreneurial businesses to thrive to become medium-sized businesses with 50 or more employees over a five-year period. The benefits from more traditional main street businesses are driven by increasing survival rates, so policies that help small businesses persevere for at least five years is much more accretive than just helping them get established. Labor policies that remove restrictions on new entrants in the workforce, reduce government size (i.e. employment) and eliminate "red-tape" on businesses will promote more positive outcomes.

Policies to increase post-secondary graduation rates as well as create, recruit, and retain a college-educated workforce will drive greater economic prosperity within any U.S. state. Our educational institutions should continue to promote entrepreneurship, but not at the exclusion of teaching invaluable and necessary skills to run and grow a small business. This study acknowledges that virtually all big businesses start as small businesses and encourages sound business practices that promote and balance both survival and growth. High school attainment by itself is not a significant influence on economic benefits, but it should be recognized as a necessary step towards achieving post-secondary education, which significantly contributes to positive entrepreneurial outcomes. Personal freedom was not statistically significant at the state level, but further consideration is warranted assuming it and other lifestyle factors may have secondary influences on, for example, recruiting and retaining the college-educated workforce businesses need to survive and grow. This dissertation challenges entrepreneurial economics by proposing a novel model based on the decomposition of the Kauffman Index of Entrepreneurial Activity and the Economic Freedom of North America to highlight specific activities and policies that can move the needle in the 21st century. The study finds that entrepreneurship accounts for 32% of the variation in state-level financial outcomes and suggests that U.S. economic prosperity requires greater main street and high-growth entrepreneurial activity, *ceteris paribus*. Furthermore, these entrepreneurial activities are highly dependent upon institutional quality, wherein labor freedom(s) are the most significant influence on prosperity at the state level.

Limitations

The objective of this study was to estimate the influences of entrepreneurial activities and supporting regulations and policies on state-level financial outcomes, not to define a complete model of REAL_GSP. Therefore, variables have been omitted by design and are a major limitation in this study. Although the results are shown to be sufficiently robust, extrapolating the impact of specific explanatory variables based on their coefficient beyond order of magnitude or relative comparison may be misleading. The overall estimate of entrepreneurship contributing 32% of the variation in real per capita gross state product is consistent with previous findings, but also highlights that a larger majority of economic outcome is undefined by the study's empirical models. Although the study uses a sufficiently large sample for robust empirical analysis, the time horizon is limited to the most recent eight years and economic trends often materialize over an even longer time horizon given that growth from new business formation may take from five to seven years to manifest (Plehn-Dujowich & Grove, 2012). Lastly, the KIEA indices do not capture the earliest and nascent entrepreneurial activity, so the findings may underreport entrepreneurial contributions that may emerge over a longer period of study.

Recommendations for Future Research

The findings of this study justify additional research to understand the causes of the recent decline in business dynamism and entrepreneurship and continue to assess these trends over a longer time horizon. Is the decline to entrepreneurial activity a result of declining economic freedom, demographic shifts or some structural change or emerging barrier to sustained entrepreneurial growth? Answering these questions should be a high priority as the consequences may have a profound impact on the United States' prosperity and standard of living at both the state and national levels. The findings suggest policymakers should focus on main street survival rates and scaling entrepreneurial growth businesses to improve financial well-being. Exactly how to advance these specific value-creating activities needs further consideration and understanding. The answer surely is not as simple as training your brain to think like Elon Musk (Gonzalez, 2016) or encouraging more MBA hackathons with cash prizes (Gee, 2018).

The decline in entrepreneurial activity may also be influenced by factors that are not represented or evident at the state level. Empirical research at the metro and regional levels may provide additional insights subject to availability of reliable and localized indicators for entrepreneurial activity, economic freedom, and economic well-being. Lastly, consideration must be given to distinct demographic changes and trends that may contribute to alternative explanations for the nation's entrepreneurial "slump"; perhaps aging baby boomers are optimizing for retirement while millennial entrepreneurs have yet to strike out on their own? The United States has tremendous entrepreneurial advantages inherent in the nation's diversity and immigration, which improve firm and national economic performance (Blau, Free, & Macmillan, 1977; Richard, Barnett, Dwyer, & Chadwick, 2004).

The United States has the greatest institutional support of entrepreneurship in the developed world, including small business financing, procurement advocacy, and small business development assistance (Parker & Parker, 2009). However, the underlying data used in this study hints at trends that pose challenges and opportunities. Entrepreneurship and outcomes lag changes in the U.S. population, which continue to both age and become increasingly diverse. Millennials start less new ventures when compared to the previous generations, *ceteris paribus*, and minorities and women are disproportionately underrepresented in the startup economy (Morelix, Hwang, & S., 2017). This study reiterates recent calls for additional research on post-retirement business entry, student loans consequences, and greater diversity and participation in entrepreneurship for continued U.S. Economic well-being (Zhang, 2018).

APPENDICES

Appendix A

Descriptive Statistics

Variable	Mean	Median	Std. Dev.	Skewness	Kurtosis
PCREAL_GSP	47265.4	46026.5	8949.1	0.672	2.947
LOG(PCREAL_GSP)	10.75	10.74	0.18	0.269	2.532
MAINSTREET_INDEX	0.31	0.21	1.39	0.310	3.727
STARTUP_INDEX	-0.46	-0.67	1.55	0.314	2.522
GROWTH_INDEX	0.37	0.32	2.10	0.703	4.402
EFNA_OVERALL_SUBN	6.88	6.91	0.59	0.072	2.775
EFNA_A1_SUBN	6.75	6.78	0.95	-0.665	3.755
EFNA_A2_SUBN	6.74	6.73	0.79	-0.081	3.736
EFNA_A3_SUBN	7.14	7.17	0.58	-0.248	2.642
UNEMP_RATE	6.42	6.18	2.03	0.668	3.253
P_BACH	28.12	27.50	4.87	0.308	2.635
P_HIGHSCHOOL	87.60	88.30	3.28	-0.434	2.110
P_ADV_DEG	10.30	9.70	2.53	0.971	3.442
POP_GROWTH					
US50_OVERALL	0.00	0.04	0.25	-1.585	6.785
US50_ECONOMIC	-0.01	0.07	0.26	-1.283	5.480
US50_FISCAL	0.02	0.02	0.14	-1.121	6.455
US50_REGULATORY	-0.03	-0.01	0.16	-0.799	3.505
US50_PERSONAL	0.01	0.00	0.08	0.233	2.461
PCPERINCOME	43133.4	41890	7423.8	0.777	3.336
RMED_HHINCOME	54633.7	53848	8672.6	0.346	2.521
JAN_TEMP	30.8	30.0	12.8	0.431	4.379
HOWN	67.9	68.7	5.1	-0.846	3.834
PER_IMMG	0.52%	0.48%	0.22%	1.049	4.589
PER_NET_MIGR	0.01%	0.13%	1.07%	-5.148	36.859
IMMG_SHARE	8.58%	6.46%	6.07%	1.107	3.497
SOPPSHARE_NEW_ENT	78.68%	78.75%	6.29%	-0.154	3.111
SRATE_NEW_ENTRP	0.30%	0.29%	0.07%	0.377	2.622
STARTUP_DENSITY	82.2	77.6	17.9	1.041	4.169
EST_SMALL_BUSDENS	631.4	639.2	48.0	-1.038	4.634
MRATE_BUS_OWNERS	6.9%	6.6%	1.7%	0.890	3.578
MSURVIVAL_RATE	46.7%	46.7%	3.6%	-0.259	3.483
GSTART_GROWTH	54.5%	53.0%	20.0%	1.936	10.893
GH_G_DENSITY	55.7	53.5	33.1	0.781	3.857
GSHARE_SCALE	1.49%	1.51%	0.33%	0.436	4.521

Variable	Description
STARTUP_INDEX	Kauffman Index of Startup Activity relies on three indicators to evaluate new business creation: the Rate of New Entrepreneurs in the economy, calculated as the percentage of adults becoming entrepreneurs in a given month; the Opportunity Share of New Entrepreneurs, calculated as the percentage of new entrepreneurs driven primarily by opportunity vs. necessity; Startup Density, the number of new employer businesses divided by the total population of existing employer businesses.
OPPSHARE_NEW_ENTRP	Opportunity Share of New Entrepreneurs —the percentage of new entrepreneurs driven primarily by "opportunity" as opposed to "necessity."
RATE_NEW_ENTRP	Rate of New Entrepreneurs -The Rate of New Entrepreneurs in the economy— the percentage of adults becoming entrepreneurs in a given month
STARTUP_DENSITY	The Startup Density of a region, measured as the number of new employer businesses, normalized by the business population.
MAINSTREET_INDEX	The Main Street Entrepreneurship Index is an indicator and equally weighted index of three normalized measures of business activity- the number of established small businesses, the survival rate of companies, and the number of business owners in a location
RATE_OF_BUSINESS_OWNERS	Main Street Component: The Rate of Business Owners in the economy, calculated as the percentage of adults owning businesses as their main jobs
EST_SMALL_BUSINESS_DENSITY	Main Street Component: The Established Small Business Density, measured as the number of established small employer businesses normalized by the total number of firms.
MSURVIVAL_RATE	Main Street Component: The Survival Rate of firms, calculated as the percentage of firms that remain in operation throughout their first five years. For instance, the 2015 cohort consists of the percentage of firms that started five years ago (in 2010) and are still in business in 2015.
GROWTH_INDEX	Kauffman Index of Growth Entrepreneurship is an equally weighted index of three normalized measures of growth consisting of; Rate of Startup Growth, Share of Scaleups, and High Growth Company Density
GSHARE_SCALE	KIEA Growth Index component, Share of Scaleups, calculated as the number of firms that started small but grew to employ fifty people or more by their tenth year of operation as a percentage of all employer firms ten years and younger.
START_GROWTH	The Rate of Startup Growth captures the average growth of all young employer businesses in the economy. calculated as how much startups have grown, on average, after five years of founding, as measured by change in employment.
H_G_DENSITY	High-Growth Company Density of a region, measured as the number of private businesses with at least $2 million in annual revenue reaching three years of 20 percent annualized revenue growth, normalized by total employer business population.

Variable	Description
EFNA_OVERALL_SUBN	Economic Freedom of North America Index - Subnational Indices across North America for US States
EFNA_A2_SUBN	Economic Freedom of North America Index - State Index Area 2 2. Taxation 2A. Income and Payroll Tax Revenue as a Percentage of Income 2Bi. Top Marginal Income Tax Rate and the Income Threshold at Which It Applies 2Bii. Top Marginal Income and Payroll Tax Rate (all-government index only, component 1Dii in EFW) 2C. Property Tax and Other Taxes as a Percentage of Income 2D. Sales Taxes as a Percentage of Income
EFNA_A3_SUBN	Economic Freedom of North America Index - State Index Area 3 3. Regulation 3A. Labor Market Freedom 3Ai. Minimum Wage Legislation 3Aii. Government Employment as a Percentage of Total State/Provincial Employment 3Aiii. Union Density 3Aiv. Hiring Regulations and Minimum Wage (all-government index only, component 5Bi in EFW) 3Av. Hiring and Firing Regulations (all-government index only, component 5Bii in EFW) 3Avi. Centralized Collective Bargaining (all-government index only, component 5Biii in EFW) 3Avii. Hours Regulations (all-government index only, component 5Biv in EFW) 3Aviii. Mandated Cost of Worker Dismissal (all-government index only, component 5Bv in EFW) 3Aix. Conscription (all-government index only, component 5Bvi in EFW) 3B. Regulation of Credit Markets (all-government index only, component 5A in EFW) 3C. Business Regulations (all-government index only, component 5C in EFW)
EFNA_OVERALL_G	Economic Freedom of North America Index - Overall Indices across North America for All Governments
EFNA_1A_SUBN	EFNA Size of Government Component - Expenditures 1A. General Consumption Expenditures by Government as a Percentage of Income
EFNA_1B_SUBN	EFNA Size of Government Component - Transfers 1B. Transfers and Subsidies as a Percentage of Income
EFNA_1C_SUBN	EFNA Size of Government Component - Insurance & Retirement 1C. Insurance and Retirement Payments as a Percentage of Income
EFNA_2A_SUBN	EFNA Taxation Component - Income & Payroll Tax 2A. Income and Payroll Tax Revenue as a Percentage of Income
EFNA_2B_SUBN	EFNA Taxation Component - Top Tax Rate 2B. Top Marginal Income Tax Rate and the Income Threshold at Which It Applies

Variable	Description
EFNA_2C_SUBN	EFNA Taxation Component - Property tax 2C. Property Tax and Other Taxes as a Percentage of Income
EFNA_2D_SUBN	EFNA Taxation Component - Sales Tax 2D. Sales Taxes as a Percentage of Income
EFNA_3AII_SUBN	EFNA Regulation Component - Government Employment Percentage 3Aii. Government Employment as a Percentage of Total State Employment
EFNA_3AIII_SUBN	EFNA Regulation Component - Union Density 3Aiii. Union Density
US50_OVERALL	The overall freedom ranking is a combination of personal and economic freedoms CATO Institute Ruger & Sorens (2016) www.freedominthe50states.org
US50_ECONOMIC	US50 Economic Freedom, CATO Institute Ruger & Sorens (2016) www.freedominthe50states.org Combined weighted of Fiscal Policy: 29.5% and Regulatory Policy: 38.7%
US50_FISCAL	U50 Fiscal Freedom CATO Institute Ruger & Sorens (2016) www.freedominthe50states.org Fiscal Policy: 29.5%-32.0%State Taxation: 13.4%Local Taxation: 78.6%-10.1%Government Subsidies: 2.3%Government debt: 2.1%
US50_PERSONAL	US50 Personal Freedom U50 Fiscal Freedom CATO Institute Ruger & Sorens (2016) www.freedominthe50states.org Incarceration and arrests: 6.6% Marriage freedom: 4.0% Education: 3.2% Gun control: 3.2% Local gun ban: 1.0% Alcohol: 2.9% Marijuana Freedom: 2.1% Gambling: 1.9% Asset forfeiture: 1.8% Tobacco 1.7% Cigarette tax: 1.3% Travel freedom: 1.4% Mala prohibita and civil liberties: 0.5% Campaign finance: 0.1%
PCPERINCOME	Annual Real Per Capita Personal Income –used as an alternative indicator of economic welfare and benchmark U.S. Dept. of Commerce U.S. Bureau of Economic Analysis, State Data
RMED_HHINCOME	Annual Real Median Household Income –used as an alternative indicator of economic welfare and benchmark U.S. Dept. of Commerce U.S. Bureau of Economic Analysis, State Data

Appendix B

Correlation Matrices

Correlation Matrix for Explanatory Variables

	PCREAL_GSP	MAINSTREET_INDEX	STARTUP_INDEX	GROWTH_INDEX	EFNA_A3_SUBN	UNEMP_RATE	P_HIGHSCHL	P_BACH
PCREAL_GSP	1							
MAINSTREET_INDEX	0.1880	1						
STARTUP_INDEX	-0.0627	0.0583	1					
GROWTH_INDEX	0.1084	-0.3915	0.0864	1				
EFNA_A3_SUBN	0.1222	-0.0017	-0.1091	0.2763	1			
UNEMP_RATE	-0.2234	-0.4684	0.0650	0.2266	-0.3537	1		
P_HIGHSCHL	0.3864	0.5324	-0.1306	-0.2415	0.0990	-0.4569	1	
P_BACH	0.5828	0.2145	-0.0992	0.2185	0.3617	-0.1749	0.4843	1

Correlation Matrix for Freedom(s)

	EFNA_A1_SUBN	EFNA_A2_SUBN	EFNA_A3_SUBN	EFNA_OVERALL_G	EFNA_OVERALL_SUBN	US50_OVERALL	US50_ECONOMIC	US50_PERSONAL	US50_FISCAL	US50_REGULATORY
EFNA_A1_SUBN	1.0000									
EFNA_A2_SUBN	0.2323	1.0000								
EFNA_A3_SUBN	0.6424	0.2535	1.0000							
EFNA_OVERALL_G	0.5917	0.2812	0.2396	1.0000						
EFNA_OVERALL_SUBN	0.8479	0.6523	0.7836	0.5197	1.0000					
US50_OVERALL	0.4031	0.7094	0.2630	0.4641	0.6172	1.0000				
US50_ECONOMIC	0.4100	0.6899	0.2532	0.4958	0.6090	0.9578	1.0000			
US50_PERSONAL	-0.1023	-0.0698	-0.0166	-0.2001	-0.0912	-0.0473	-0.3323	1.0000		
US50_FISCAL	0.4654	0.8096	0.4488	0.4168	0.7560	0.8397	0.8452	-0.1819	1.0000	
US50_REGULATORY	0.2608	0.4159	0.0213	0.4416	0.3314	0.8233	0.8867	-0.3802	0.5023	1.0000

Correlation Matrix for KIEA Subnational Indices

	STARTUP INDEX	STARTUP_DENSITY	SRATE_NEW ENTRP	SOPPSHARE_NEW ENTRP	MAINSTREET INDEX	SURVIVAL RATE	MRATE_OF_BUSOWNER	EST_SMALL_BUS_DENS	GROWTH INDEX	GSTART GROWTH	GSHARE SCALE	GH_G_DENSITY
STARTUP_INDEX	1.0000											
STARTUP_DENSITY	0.6581	1.0000										
RATE_NEW_ENTRP	0.8652	0.4029	1.0000									
SOPPSHARE_NEW_ENTRP	0.3629	0.0475	-0.0332	1.0000								
MAINSTREET_INDEX	0.0437	-0.2697	0.0149	0.3370	1.0000							
SURVIVAL_RATE	-0.0452	-0.1249	-0.1983	0.3886	0.7950	1.0000						
RATE_OF_BUSOWNERS	0.4821	0.2545	0.4161	0.2351	0.7185	0.3318	1.0000					
EST_SMALL_BUS_DENS	-0.6086	-0.9333	-0.3809	-0.0194	0.3628	0.2073	-0.2148	1.0000				
GROWTH_INDEX	0.0691	0.4311	-0.0794	-0.0533	-0.3850	-0.0683	-0.2624	-0.4641	1.0000			
GSTART_GROWTH	0.2882	0.3740	0.1768	0.0792	-0.1301	-0.0243	0.0516	-0.3810	0.6418	1.0000		
GSHARE_SCALE	-0.0608	0.2512	-0.1966	-0.0037	-0.3623	0.0016	-0.3288	-0.3884	0.6731	0.3103	1.0000	
GH_G_DENSITY	-0.0577	0.2651	-0.1280	-0.1449	-0.2916	-0.0982	-0.2447	-0.2185	0.7220	0.1101	0.1869	1.0000

REFERENCES

Acs, Z. J., Audretsch, D. B., & Feldman, M. P. (1994). R & D spillovers and recipient firm size. *The Review of Economics and Statistics, 76*(2), 336-340.

Backhaus, J. R. G., & Schumpeter, J. A. (2003). Joseph Alois Schumpeter : Entrepreneurship, style, and vision.

Baughn, C. C., Neupert, K. E., & Sugheir, J. S. (2013). Domestic migration and new business creation in the United States. *Journal of Small Business and Entrepreneurship, 26*(1), 1-14.

Baumol, W. J. (1990). Entrepreneurship: Productive, unproductive, and destructive. *Journal of Political Economy, 98*(5), 893-921.

Baumol, W. J. (2002). Entrepreneurship: Productive, unproductive, and destructive. *Foundations of Entrepreneurship.*

Beaulier, S., & Sutter, D. (2013). Entrepreneurship and the link between economic freedom and growth. *American Journal of Entrepreneurship, 6*(1), 1-11.

Bjørnskov, C., & Foss, N. (2008). Economic freedom and entrepreneurial activity: Some cross-country evidence. *Public Choice, 134*(3-4), 3-4.

Bjørnskov, C., & Foss, N. (2013). How strategic entrepreneurship and the institutional context drive economic growth. *Strategic Entrepreneurship Journal, 7*(1), 50-69.

Bjørnskov, C., & Foss, N. J. (2016). Institutions, entrepreneurship, and economic growth: What do we know and what do we still need to know? *The Academy of Management Perspectives, 30*(3), 292.

Blau, P. M., Free, P., & Macmillan, C. (1977). *Inequality and heterogeneity : A primitive theory of social structure.* New York; London: Free Press ; Collier Macmillan Publishers.

Bo, C., Pontus, B., Maureen, M., Christer, O., Lars, P., & HÂkan, Y. (2013). The evolving domain of entrepreneurship research. *Small Business Economics, 41*(4), 913-930.

Bradley, S. W., & Klein, P. (2016). Institutions, economic freedom, and entrepreneurship: The

    contribution of management scholarship. *Academy of Management Perspectives, 30*(3),

    211-221. doi:10.5465/amp.2013.0137

Burgelman, R. A. (1983). A process model of internal corporate venturing in the diversified major

    firm. *Administrative Science Quarterly, 28*(2), 223-244.

Burger, J. D., & Schwartz, J. S. (2018). Jobless recoveries: Stagnation or structural change?

    Economic Inquiry, 56(2), 709-723. doi:http://dx.doi.org/10.1111/ecin.12535

Campbell, N., Mitchell, D. T., & Rogers, T. M. (2013a). Multiple measures of US entrepreneurial

    activity and classical liberal institutions. *Journal of Entrepreneurship and Public Policy,*

    2(1), 4-20. doi:http://dx.doi.org/10.1108/20452101311318648

Campbell, N., Mitchell, D. T., & Rogers, T. M. (2013b). Multiple measures of US entrepreneurial

    activity and classical liberal institutions. *Journal of Entrepreneurship and Public Policy,*

    2(1), 4-20.

Campbell, N. D., & Rogers, T. M. (2007). Economic freedom and net business formation. *Cato*

    Journal, 27(1), 23-36.

Casson, M. (1982). *The entrepreneur : An economic theory.* Totowa, N.J.: Barnes & Noble Books.

Cebula, R. J. (2014). The impact of economic freedom and personal freedom on net in-migration

    in the U.S.: A state-level empirical analysis, 2000 to 2010. *Journal of Labor Research,*

    35(1), 88-103.

Cebula, R. J., Hall, J. C., Mixon, F. G., & Payne, J. E. (2015). *Economic behavior, economic*

    freedom, and entrepreneurship.

Cheung, O. L. (2014). Impact of innovative environment on economic growth: An examination of

    state per capita GDP and personal income. *Journal of Business & Economics Research,*

    12(3), 257.

Crossan, M. M., & Apaydin, M. (2010). A multi-dimensional framework of organizational innovation: A systematic review of the literature. *Journal of Management Studies, 47*(6), 1154-1191.

Cunningham, J. B., & Lischeron, J. (1991). Defining entrepreneurship. *Journal of Small Business Management, 29*(1), 45-61.

Decker, R., Haltiwanger, J., Jarmin, R., & Miranda, J. (2014). The role of entrepreneurship in US job creation and economic dynamism. *The Journal of Economic Perspectives, 28*(3), 3-24.

Decker, R. A., Haltiwanger, J., Jarmin, R. S., & Miranda, J. (2016a). New developments in firm dynamics in understanding business dynamism, declining business dynamism, declining business dynamism: What we know and the way forward. *The American Economic Review, 106*(5), 203-207.

Decker, R. A., Haltiwanger, J., Jarmin, R. S., & Miranda, J. (2016b). Where has all the skewness gone? The decline in high-growth (young) firms in the U.S. *European Economic Review, 86*, 4-23.

Díaz-Casero, J. C., Coduras, A., & Hernández-Mogollón, R. (2012). Economic freedom and entrepreneurial activity. *Management Decision, 50*(9), 1686-1711.

Drucker, P. F. (1985/06/May). The discipline of innovation. *Harvard Business Review, 63,* 67.

Gartner, W. B., Carland, J. W., Hoy, F., & Carland, J. A. C. (1988). 'Who Is An Entrepreneur?' Is the wrong question. *American Journal of Small Business, 12*(4), 11.

Gee, K. (2018). M.B.A. students compete for cash in rapid-pitch contests.

Gonzalez, G. (2016). How Elon Musk trains his brain for greatness.

Griliches, Z., Engle, R. F., Intriligator, M. D., & McFadden, D. (1983). *Handbook of econometrics*: Elsevier.

Gwartney, J. (2009). Institutions, economic freedom, and cross-country differences in performance. *Southern Economic Journal, 75*(4), 937-956.

Gwartney, J., Lawson, R., & Hall, J. (2017). Economic freedom of the world : 2017 annual report.

Gwartney, J. D., Holcombe, R. G., & Lawson, R. A. (2004). Economic freedom, institutional

quality, and cross-country differences in income and growth. *Cato Journal, 24*(3), 205-233.

Gwartney, J. D., Lawson, R., Block, W., & Fraser, I. (1996). *Economic freedom of the world,*

1975-1995. [Vancouver, B.C.]: Fraser Institute.

Hafer, R. W. (2013). Entrepreneurship and state economic growth. *Journal of Entrepreneurship*

and Public Policy, 2(1), 67-79. doi:http://dx.doi.org/10.1108/20452101311318684

Hair, J. F., Black, W. C., Babin, B. J., Anderson, R. E., & Tatham, R. L. (2006). Multivariate data

analysis 6th ed. *Uppersaddle River: Pearson Prentice Hall.*

Hall, J. C., & Lawson, R. A. (2014). Economic freedom of the world: An accounting of the

literature. *Contemporary Economic Policy, 32*(1), 1-19.

Hall, J. C., Nikolaev, B., Pulito, J. M., & Van Metre, B. J. (2013). The effect of personal and

economic freedom on entrepreneurial activity: Evidence from a new state level freedom

index. *American Journal of Entrepreneurship, 6*(1), 88-103.

Hall, J. C., & Sobel, R. S. (2008). Institutions, entrepreneurship, and regional differences in

economic growth. *Southern Journal of Entrepreneurship, 1*(1).

Haltiwanger, J. C., Jarmin, R. S., & Miranda, J. (2012). Business dynamics statistics briefing:

Where have all the young firms gone? *SSRN Electronic Journal.*

Hathaway, I., & Litan, R. (2014). The other aging of America: The increasing dominance of older

firms. *Brookings Institution.*

Hausman, J. A. (1978). Specification tests in econometrics. *Econometrica: Journal of the*

econometric society, 1251-1271.

Heckman, J. J. (2000). Causal parameters and policy analysis in economics: A twentieth century retrospective. *The Quarterly Journal of Economics, 115*(1), 45-97.

Holcombe, R. G. (1998). Entrepreneurship and economic growth. *The Quarterly Journal of Austrian Economics, 1*(2), 45-62.

Hult, G. T. M., & Ketchen, D. J. (2001). Does market orientation matter?: A test of the relationship between positional advantage and performance. *Strategic Management Journal, 22*(9), 899-906.

Hurley, R. F., & Hult, G. T. M. (1998). Innovation, market orientation, and organizational learning: An integration and empirical examination. *Journal of Marketing, 62*(3), 42-54.

IHS. (2018). Retrieved from http://www.eviews.com/

Ireland, R. D., Hitt, M. A., & Sirmon, D. G. (2003). A model of strategic entrepreneurship: The construct and its dimensions. *Journal of Management, 29*(6), 963-989.

Jaworski, B. J., & Kohli, A. K. (1993). Market orientation: Antecedents and consequences. *Journal of Marketing, 57*(3), 53.

Kirzner, I. M. (1973). *Competition and entrepreneurship.* Chicago: University of Chicago Press.

Knight, G. A., & Cavusgil, S. T. (2004). Innovation, organizational capabilities, and the born-global firm. *Journal of International Business Studies, 35*(2), 124-141.

Krichevskiy, D., & Snyder, T. (2015). U.S. State Government policies and entrepreneurship.

Lepore, J. (2018). What the Gospel of Innovation Gets Wrong. *New Yorker.*

Lu, X., & White, H. (2014). Robustness checks and robustness tests in applied economics. *Journal of Econometrics, 178*, 194.

Mann, J., & Shideler, D. (2015). Measuring Schumpeterian activity using a composite indicator. *Journal of Entrepreneurship and Public Policy, 4*(1), 57-84.

Matsuno, K., Mentzer, J. T., & Ozsomer, A. (2002). The effects of entrepreneurial proclivity and market orientation on business performance. *Journal of Marketing, 66*(3), 18-32.

McKenzie, B., Ugbah, S. D., & Smothers, N. (2007). "Who Is and Entrepreneur?" Is it still the wrong question? *Academy of Entrepreneurship Journal, 13*(1), 23-43.

Miller, T., Kim, A. B., & Roberts, J. M. (2018). *Index of economic freedom 2018.* Washington; New Yord: The Heritage Foundation ; The Wall Street Journal.

Morelix, A., & Russell-Fritch. (2018). Kauffman Index Data Source.

Morelix, A., & Russell-Fritch, J. (2017). Kauffman Index 2017: Growth Entrepreneurship State Trends. *SSRN Electronic Journal.*

Morelix, A., Hwang, V., & S., T. I. (2017). 2017 State of entrepreneurship report zero barriers: Three mega trends shaping the future of entrepreneurship. *Electronic Journal.* Retrieved from https://www.kauffman.org/

Narver, J. C., & Slater, S. F. (1990). The effect of a market orientation on business profitability. *Journal of Marketing, 54*(4), 20.

Network, U. (2018). Why millennials choose to join corporate America over becoming entrepreneurs.

North, D. (1990). Institutions and their consequences for economic performance. *The Limits of Rationality*, 383-401.

North, D. C. (1991). Institutions. *Journal of economic perspectives, 5*(1), 97-112.

Oulton, N. (2012). Hooray for GDP!

Parker, S. C. (2004). *The economics of self-employment and entrepreneurship*: Cambridge University Press.

Parker, S. C. (2005). The economics of entrepreneurship: What we know and what we don't. *Foundations and Trends in Entrepreneurship, 1*(1), 1-54.

Parker, S. C., & Parker, S. C. (2009). The economics of entrepreneurship.

Pearson, D., Nyonna, D., & Kim, K.-J. (2012). The relationship between economic freedom, state growth and foreign direct investment in US States. *International Journal of Economics and Finance, 4*(10), 140.

Plehn-Dujowich, J. M., & Grove, W. (2012). The dynamic relationship between entrepreneurship, unemployment, and growth: Evidence from US industries. *Plehn Analytical Economic Solutions, LLC, Willow Grove. Under contract number SBAHQ-10-M-0204.*

Powell, B., & Weber, R. (2013). Economic freedom and entrepreneurship: A panel study of the United States. *American Journal of Entrepreneurship, 6*(1), 67-87.

Rich, R. (2018). *The Great Recession.*

Richard, O. C., Barnett, T., Dwyer, S., & Chadwick, K. (2004). Cultural diversity in management, Firm performance, and the moderating role of entrepreneual orientation dimensions. *The Academy of Management Journal, 47*(2), 255-266. doi:10.2307/20159576

Ruger, W., & Sorens, J. (2017a). *Freedom in the 50 states : An index of personal and economic freedom.*

Ruger, W., & Sorens, J. (2017b). *Freedom in the 50 states : An index of personal and economic freedom dataset* [excel].

Ruger, W. P., & Sorens, J. (2017). *Freedom in the 50 States: An index of personal and economic freedom*: Cato Institute.

Russell, J., Morelix, A., Fairlie, R. W., & Reedy, E. J. (2015). The Kauffman Index 2015: Main street entrepreneurship state trends. *SSRN Electronic Journal.*

Russell, J., Morelix, A., Fairlie, R. W., & Reedy, E. J. (2016). The Kauffman Index 2016: Startup activity state trends. *SSRN Electronic Journal.*

Salanti, A., Marchi, N. D., & Blaug, M. (1992). Appraising economic theories: Studies in the methodology of research programs. *The Economic Journal The Economic Journal, 102*(415), 1534.

Scott, S., & Venkataraman, S. (2001). Entrepreneurship as a field of research: A response to Zahra and Dess, Singh, and Erickson. *Academy of Management. The Academy of Management Review, 26*(1), 13-16.

Sobel, R. S. (2008). Testing Baumol: Institutional quality and the productivity of entrepreneurship. *Journal of Business Venturing, 23*(6), 641-655.

Stansel, D., Torra, J., & McMahon, F. (2017). Economic freedom of North America 2017.

Stead, W. E., Worrell, D. L., & Stead, J. G. (1990). An integrative model for understanding and managing ethical behavior in business organizations. *Journal of Business Ethics, 9*(3), 233-242. doi:10.2307/25072030

United, S., & Bureau of Economic, A. (2006). Gross domestic product by state estimation methodology.

Wiseman, T., & Young, A. T. (2013). Economic freedom, entrepreneurship, & income levels: Some US state-level empirics. *American Journal of Entrepreneurship, 6*(1), 104-124.

Worstall, T. (2018). US jobless claims fall to lowest rate ever - at least since records began.

Zahra, S. A., & Wright, M. (2011). Entrepreneurship's next act. *The Academy of Management Perspectives, 25*(4), 67-83.

Zhang, T. (2018). Age and entrepreneurship.

CPSIA information can be obtained
at www.ICGtesting.com
Printed in the USA
BVHW011620211119
564447BV00002B/23/P